WOMEN
OF THE
WORD

BIBLE
STUDY
SERIES

FREE
FROM
WORRY

JANICE WISE

Gospel Light

Published by Gospel Light
Ventura, California, U.S.A.
www.gospellight.com
Printed in the U.S.A.

Aglow International is an interdenominational organization of
Christian women and men. Our mission is to lead the lost to Jesus Christ and provide
opportunity for believers to grow in their faith and minister to others.
Our publications are used to help women and men find a personal relationship with
Jesus Christ, to enhance growth in their Christian experience, and to help them
recognize their roles and relationships according to Scripture. For more
information about our organization, please write to Aglow International,
P.O. Box 1749, Edmonds, WA 98020-1749, U.S.A., or call (425) 775-7282.
For ordering or information about the Aglow studies and other
resources, visit the Aglow e-store at www.aglow.org.

CONTENTS

OREWORD

When the apostle Paul poured out his heart in letters to the young churches in Asia, he was responding to his apostolic call to shepherd those tender flocks. They needed encouragement in their new life in Jesus. They needed solid doctrine. They needed truth from someone who had an intimate relationship with God and with them.

Did Paul know as he was writing that these simple letters would form the bulk of the New Testament? We can be confident that the Holy Spirit did! How like God to use Paul's relationship with these churches to cement His plan and purpose in their lives, and, generations later, in ours.

We in Aglow can relate to Paul's desire to bond those young churches together in the faith. After 1967, when Aglow fellowships began bubbling up across the United States and in other countries, they needed encouragement. They needed to know the fullness of who they were in Christ. They needed relationship. Like Paul, our desire to reach out and nurture from far away birthed a series of Bible studies that have fed thousands since 1973 when our first study, *Genesis*, was published. Our studies share heart to heart, giving Christians new insights about themselves and their relationship with and in God.

In 1998, God's generous nature provided us a rewarding new relationship with Gospel Light. Together we published our Aglow classics as well as a selection of exciting new studies. Gospel Light began as a publishing ministry much in the same way Aglow began publishing Bible studies. Henrietta Mears formed Gospel Light in response to requests from churches across America for the Sunday School materials she had written. Gospel Light remains a strong ministry-minded witness for the gospel around the world.

Our heart's desire is that these studies will continue to kindle the minds of women and men, touch their hearts, and refresh their spirits with the light and life a loving Savior abundantly supplies.

This study, *Free from Worry* by Janice Wise, will expose the source of anxiety and guide you along God's path out of the deadly habit of worry and into the joy and peace He has promised to all who believe.

Jane Hansen-Hoyt
International President
Aglow International

NTRODUCTION

Worry, worry, worry. For too many of us, worry is an evil "dis-ease" invading our minds and bodies, spreading its tentacles throughout our lives until it saps our spiritual power and joy.

Today, anxiety is an accepted part of the cost of living in the human race. We are bombarded with stress relievers, relaxation techniques and meditation practices to help ease the strain of worry's side effects.

Many Christians worry more than those who have no relationship with God. We know too much in our heads and believe too little in our hearts. In the gap between what we know and what we truly believe, worry breeds.

Because we are children of our father Adam and have inherited his sin nature, our minds provide the perfect soil in which anxiety can grow. However, the Bible tells us that when we come into the family of God we are born anew. According to Scripture, our new birth changes us from self-centered to God-centered creatures. Why, then, do we still worry?

Salvation through Jesus Christ takes us out of worry; that same salvation can take the worry out of us—if we will let it. We *are* new creatures, but many of us still entertain our old-creature thought patterns. Like a pair of everyday shoes, worry has been our everyday way of thinking, a part of our comfort zone. One person contemplating the value of the *Free from Worry* study wondered aloud, "What would I think about if I didn't worry?"

Sometimes we feel that worry enhances our concerned-Christian image. The more we worry, the more we appear to care. Yet once anxiety has established a stronghold in our lives, it robs us of faith, turning true compassion into a self-preserving concern. We become "worried witnesses," and the world finds little in our anxious behavior to draw them to the One we call Lord.

The purpose of *Free from Worry* is to look at the truth about anxiety and then let that truth change your life. The process involves a faith walk, but just think what your life would be like if you were free from the crippling effects of worry.

Take the time to go through this study and experience the release offered. You will taste freedom and see that whomever the Son sets free from worry is free indeed.

An Overview of the Study

This Bible study is divided into four sections:

1. *A Closer Look at the Problem* defines the problem and the goal of the lesson.

2. *A Closer Look at God's Truth* gets you into God's Word. What does God have to say about the problem? How can you begin to apply God's Word as you work through each lesson?

3. *A Closer Look at My Own Heart* will help you clarify and further apply biblical truths in your own life. It will also give guidance as you work toward change.

4. *Action Steps I Can Take Today* is designed to help you concentrate on immediate steps of action.

What You Will Need

- *A Bible*—The main Bible version used in this study is the *New International Version,* but you can use whatever Bible translation you are used to reading.

- *A Notebook*—During this study you will want to keep a journal to record what God shows you personally. You may also want to journal additional thoughts or feelings that come up as you go through the lessons. Some questions may require more space than is given in this study book.

- *Time to Meditate*—Only through meditation on what you're learning will you hear God's Word for you and begin to experience a heart knowledge, as well as a head knowledge, of the subject of being free from worry. Give the Holy Spirit time to personalize His Word to your heart so that you can know what your response should be to the knowledge you are gaining.

How to Start and Lead A Small Group

One key to leading a small group is to ask yourself, *What would Jesus do and how would He do it?* Jesus began His earthly ministry with a small group called the disciples, and the fact of His presence made wherever He was a safe place to be. Think of a small group as a safe place. It is a place that reflects God's heart and His hands. The way in which Jesus lived and worked with His disciples is a basic small-group model that we are able to draw both direction and nurture from.

Paul exhorted us to "walk in love, as Christ also has loved us and given Himself for us" (Ephesians 5:2, *NKJV*). We, as His earthly reflections, are privileged to walk in His footsteps, to help bind up the brokenhearted as He did or simply to listen with a compassionate heart. Whether you use this book as a Bible study, or as a focus point for a support group, a church group or a home group, walking in love means that we "bear one another's burdens" (Galatians 6:2, *NKJV*). The loving atmosphere provided by a small group can nourish, sustain and lift us up as nothing else can.

Jesus walked in love and spoke from an honest heart. In His endless well of compassion He never misplaced truth. Rather, He surrounded it with mercy. Those who left His presence felt good about themselves because Jesus used truth to point them in the right direction for their lives. When He spoke about the sinful woman who washed Jesus' feet with her tears and wiped them with her hair, He did not deny her sin. He said, "Her sins, which are many, are forgiven, for she loved much" (Luke 7:47, *NKJV*). That's honesty without condemnation.

Jesus was a model of servant leadership (see Mark 10:43-44). One of the key skills a group leader possesses is the ability to be an encourager of the group's members to grow spiritually. Keeping in personal contact with each member of the group, especially if one is absent, tells each one that he or she is important to the group. Other skills an effective group leader demonstrates include being a good listener, guiding the discussion, as well as guiding the group to deal with any conflicts that arise within it.

Whether you're a veteran or brand new to small-group leadership, virtually every group you lead will be different in personality and dynamic. The constant is the presence of Jesus Christ, and when He is at the group's center, everything else will come together.

YOU'RE INVITED!

TO GROW . . .

To develop and reach maturity; thrive; to spring up;
come into existence from a source;

WITH A GROUP . . .

An assemblage of persons gathered or located together;
a number of individuals considered together because of similarities;

TO EXPLORE . . .

To investigate systematically; examine; search into or range over
for the purpose of discovery;

NEW TOPICS

Subject of discussion or conversation.

MEETING

Date _____ Time _____

Place: _____

_____

Contact : _____

Phone: _____

Making a Choice

The worried cow would have lived 'til now
If she had saved her breath.
But she feared her hay wouldn't last all day
So she mooed herself to death.

AUTHOR UNKNOWN

We laugh at the silliness of the cow described in this poem, but how many times have we allowed worry to kill our joy, our peace, our faith and maybe even our health? Have you ever confessed, "I'm worried sick about _health_"?

The medical profession quotes alarming statistics concerning the number of anxiety-related ailments, and most of us know from personal experience how worry magnifies the difficulties of our already-existing physical problems.

Can we really be free from the anxieties that work so much destruction in our lives? The Word of God says that not only can we live free from the worry lies that seek to imprison our minds and hearts, but that as children of the heavenly Father, we also are *expected* to live free. We *do* have a choice.

Before going on, take a moment to pray: "Lord, help me to see worry as You see it. Make me aware that I do have a choice, and show me how to become free from worry's destructive pattern in my life. Amen."

A Closer Look at the Problem

We can be free from the worry that saps both our physical strength and our spiritual power. In this first chapter, we'll look at the source of anxiety: Where did it start and where does it come from today? Discovering the root of the problem will help us recognize the choice available to us as children of God.

In Hosea 4:6, God says, "My people are destroyed from lack of knowledge." Notice that God says this of *His* people. We can be Christians and still not know how to walk in the freedom God has provided for us in Jesus Christ.

A Closer Look at God's Truth

After their creation, Adam and Eve walked in close fellowship with God. God enjoyed the humans He had created in His image, and He intended for them to know Him in an intimate way. He planned to help them grow in their understanding of His ways, so they could rule their world with wisdom and compassion.

God gave Adam and Eve a choice in the relationship. He did not want His created ones forced to fellowship with Him or to become like Him. With all His loving heart, God wanted Adam and Eve to want to know and become like their Creator because they *chose* to do so.

When God told Adam they were free to eat from every tree in the garden except one—the Tree of the Knowledge of Good and Evil—God left His humans with a choice. Into this arena of choice, Satan came to tempt Adam and Eve. He wanted them to choose his way rather than God's. Then he would control not only the humans but also the world that God had given them to rule.

Read Genesis 3:1-7. How did Satan draw Eve into a discussion about her choice?

He became a serpent and caused her to doubt God. He told her he had unworthy motives.

What did Satan imply about the character of God as he encouraged Eve to question God's motives?

His motives were to make them believe God wanted her to be like Him and see good & evil

Although the serpent contradicted God's words of warning and implied God had lied, Eve continued to listen. Satan seemed to want prosperity for Adam and Eve and encouraged them to take the first easy step immediately. What if God were withholding something wonderful from them? Or even if He did intend to make them like Him someday, why wait? Why not have all that knowledge now? Surely God would understand and maybe even be pleased when He saw how much they had learned.

According to verse 6, what reasons for disobeying God did Eve give?

It was pleasing to the eye, desirable for gaining wisdom.

Eve's reasons sound quite rational, just like the reasons we might use today to excuse our decision for doing differently than what God commands in His Word. What do you think would have happened if Eve had taken the time to consult God before she and Adam ate the fruit?

I think she would have been reassured that he had his reasons and would have not done it

It helps to remember that in every contest where Satan enters our arenas of choice, there are three votes cast. God always votes for us, Satan always votes against us, and we get to cast the deciding vote. We know God would have helped Adam and Eve make the right choice—if they had asked Him.

Satan himself had once tried to be like God and was thrown out of heaven for his rebellion (see Isaiah 14:12-15). In his desire for revenge, he wanted to break down Adam and Eve's relationship with God and bring both them and their world under his dominion.

Now read Genesis 3:8-9. What did Adam and Eve do when they heard God walking in the Garden? Why did they do it?

They hid in the trees because they were naked and afraid.

The fear that Adam and Eve felt was not the reverent or awesome fear that comes from a healthy relationship with God. The fear they experienced came from a sense of separation from God, a knowing that they had broken fellowship by disobeying the One who created them. Fear forms the nucleus of worry, so we can imagine the anxiety with which Adam and Eve waited for God to approach them.

As they hid after eating the forbidden fruit, Adam and Eve's conversation might have gone something like this:

> *Adam:* My stomach feels funny, like I swallowed a bunch of butterflies.
>
> *Eve:* Mine, too. I wonder what's wrong with us.
>
> *Adam:* I don't know. I've never felt like this before. Maybe it's something we ate.

Adam and Eve had never experienced sinful fear and its accompanying worry, until they turned their allegiance from God to Satan. Today we know the strange, physical sensations didn't come from what they had eaten but from what was eating them. They were experiencing the death-working effects of sin.

Why do you think God asked Adam and Eve where they were (see verse 9)? Didn't He know?

God knew where they were but He asked to confirm that they had eaten the fruit and they were ashamed because they disobeyed God's rules.

Just as God questioned Adam and Eve so that they would identify where they were, you may hear God asking, "Where are you? Are you afraid? Are you worried?" He asks, not because He doesn't know, but to give you an opportunity to recognize and confess where you are so that He can begin to set you free.

A Closer Look at My Own Heart

We might wonder how Adam and Eve could be misled by Satan when they had such a close relationship with God. But Satan is the master of deceit. Paul wrote, "For Satan himself masquerades as an angel of light" (2 Corinthians 11:14). Satan has a way of making the commands of God look foolish and impractical in the reality of our circumstances.

One man quipped, "Even God would worry if He watched the evening news." Would He? How do you think God wants us to respond (see Matthew 24:6)?

Jesus said these thing will happen but the end will still come

Read Luke 10:38-42. What does Martha say to Jesus about Mary's ignoring all the preparations that seemed to need immediate attention?

Martha said Mary has left me to do all the chores. Make her come & help me.

Do you think Martha expected Jesus to agree with her once she had pointed out the problem? Why?

Martha did think Jesus would help her sime to was trying to make him comfortable, and Mary was just listening to him doing nothing.

Most worriers, especially women who worry, are uncomfortable with this passage of Scripture. We tend to think that Jesus didn't understand Martha, that He didn't appreciate the responsibility of having a house full of people and the challenge of planning meals. Being a man, perhaps Jesus could not relate to the frustration of having a sister who sat around listening to the company instead of helping with the work. We can be quite sure Martha wouldn't have complained to Jesus about the situation if she hadn't expected He would quickly correct it once He understood the problem.

Think of some situations where you have felt that God didn't understand your circumstances. Identify some times when you pointed out to Him the need as you saw it, expecting that somehow, once you explained, He would do what you thought needed to be done. What happened?

When I was alone & things seemed like they were more than I could handle. I needed someone in my family to help yet - None stepped forward. I now believe it was because I need to find myself and realize my own self worth.

According to verse 40, what was happening to Martha because of her anxiety about the preparations? From what was she being distracted (see verse 39)?

Mary was just listening to Jesus.

In His love for Martha, Jesus revealed to her a need in her life that went much deeper than her distress about serving. What did He want her to see?

That she was trying to please him.

Jesus' final words to Martha point out the fact that we have a choice. Sometimes people explain this passage of Scripture by saying Mary was a woman of prayer, a meditative personality, while Martha was a doer who would find it unthinkable to sit when work demanded her attention. However, sitting versus doing isn't the issue here. It's not a question of temperamental preference but of what or who is the focal point of our lives.

What does Jesus say about Mary's choice in this situation?

Mary had the better choice, and it would not be taken away from her.

SC pg 1593 what does it mean.

Twice Jesus had fed 4,000 to 5,000 people with a few loaves and fishes, so He could easily take care of lunch if it became a problem. Jesus wanted Martha to come to know Him and His words, so she could be set free from the distraction of worry in her life.

In Deuteronomy 8:3, God said to the Israelites, "Man does not live on bread alone but on every word that comes from the mouth of the LORD." How does Jesus illustrate this truth in His sharing with Martha and Mary?

Bread sustains but does not guarantee life, which is God's gift to those who trust in him + live by his words, commandments and promises.

The only way to become free from worry is to move into a deeper relationship with God. Adam and Eve chose to move away from their relationship with God and became anxious, fearful beings. Mary chose to move toward God by deepening her relationship with Jesus. We who identify (and even sympathize) with Martha are being challenged as she was to exchange our worry-centered thoughts for God-centered thoughts. Are *you* ready to start taking steps to be free from worry? *Yes*

Action Steps I Can Take Today

Is God asking, "Where are you?" as He seeks time with you? Is He saying, *Dorothy* [insert your name], you are worried and troubled about many things"? In the space below or on a separate piece of paper, make a list of your current worries. One woman who claimed there wouldn't be enough paper for her long list began by grouping her anxieties into categories such as children, job, church, money, and so forth. Regardless of how you choose to do it, be specific in your listing. *Satan*

Trying to be a good G.M. to all the Grandchildren
Dick + his health and driving
Keeping my mouth closed about things
that really are not my business.
I think about my future + the career
but I would not call it a worry

Now read through your list and say of each anxiety, "I realize Satan, not God, is the source of my worry about _____ [name the anxiety]." Just saying the truth out loud notifies Satan that you're aware of his working to get you to deny God's faithfulness. Write "Jesus" across your confessed worries in large letters, so that it spans the whole list. Whenever you look at your list, this will remind you that you have a choice, and because of Jesus, you can refuse to let worry run your life. (*Note:* Keep this list handy for the Action Steps section in chapter 2.)

At the end of the first session of a *Free from Worry* study, an older woman came to me and said, "I know God expects me to worry about my children and family. When you get a little older, you'll understand." She didn't come back for the rest of the study sessions.

Now I am a little older and what I understand is that this concerned woman felt it was part of God's role for her to worry about her loved ones. It was to her a purpose for living, and the study was threatening to take away that purpose. Instead of choosing to draw closer to God and His Word, she chose to protect her pattern of worry-caring for her family.

In the next chapter, we'll spend some time identifying and defining worry and learning how it differs from the compassionate caring God expects us to have for others.

$\mathscr{I}$DENTIFYING WORRY

"Why are you so worried?" Andy asked his wife.
"Who's worried?" she replied. "I'm just concerned."

Sound familiar? Most of us who know we are classic worriers also know that worry doesn't qualify as a Christian virtue. But concern? Of course, any caring person would be concerned. So we camouflage our worry with the acceptable label "concern" and continue on our worrying way—free from the stigma of being considered a worrier.

But fooling ourselves doesn't work, especially when we draw near to God for help with the disturbing situation. If we allow Him to help us recognize our fretting attitude, we realize that what we thought of as concern or compassion is really a self-centered need to have things the way we want them. Perhaps this attitude is best defined as "perverted concern."

Before we look closer at the problem, let's pray: "Lord, please help me identify the worry in my life, so I can learn how to break its destructive pattern. Amen."

A Closer Look at the Problem

Some of us are chronic worriers. It's been a way of life for us as long as we can remember. As a child, I watched my mother pace back and forth from the window to the kitchen while she waited for my father to get home for lunch. Dad was late again. It was a pattern in our life—Dad was always late and Mom always worried about him.

One day I asked, "Mom, does worrying about Dad get him home sooner?"

She looked at me in amazement. "Of course not," she replied, "but someone has to do the worrying around here."

Since my mother read her Bible and attended church regularly, I assumed she knew God needed people "to do the worrying around here" and decided I could be one of those faithful to fulfilling the task. Not until 30 years later did I recognize the truth: My worrying was not a form of godly caring. What a shock to discover that my years of strain and struggle as a dedicated worrier were years of working against God rather than with Him.

Worry is a prevailing attitude both inside and outside of the Christian community. But within the Church, we tend to be dishonest in our assessment of its presence.

One pastor said, "Don't turn all my Marthas into Marys or we'll never get anything done around here." In further conversation, he revealed that for prayer and meditation, he looked to the women he regarded as Marys; for service and accomplishment, he looked to the Marthas. As we talked, he admitted that the women he preferred to head up church committees were often the worriers in the congregation—they were motivated to get things done so that they wouldn't have to worry about them anymore.

Unless we are willing to identify worry, it will have its destructive way in our lives, regardless of whether we are mediators or go-getters by temperament. For instance, we believe we pray in faith, but is it possible we really intercede out of worry? Could much of our prayer be "worry on its knees," going to God as Martha went to Jesus, complaining and pointing out what needs to be done? One man commented, "So worry-motivated praying might be described as prayer to the wrong god." It's a startling thought: Could our fretting attitudes in prayer actually give glory to Satan?

A Closer Look at God's Truth

Each of us worries about different things. I get anxious when I hear a strange noise under the hood of my car. My husband says, "If something's wrong, when it breaks down, I'll fix it. Don't be such a worrier."

Yet my husband frets when the pile of papers on his desk gets more than a half-inch high. He hates to file and thinks the growing pile will take him all day. Then it's my turn to say, "Don't be silly; your little pile is nothing to worry about. I'll have it filed in no time."

The question isn't what we worry about, or even how much, but *why* we give worry any place at all in our lives.

In John 10:10 we read these words of Jesus: "The thief comes only to steal and kill and destroy; I have come that they may have life, and have it to the full." The thief is Satan. Since his deception of Adam and Eve in the Garden where he *stole* control of the world through Adam and Eve's rebellion, Satan continues to try to *kill* any intimate relationship between God and man. He seeks to *destroy* us and the earth, plotting to infiltrate with evil all that God called good.

Consider this: Does worry add abundance to your life, or does it take it away? List some of the ways that worry steals, kills and destroys in your life (e.g., steals sleep, kills appetite, destroys peace of mind, and so forth).

Steals my sleep - Puts a lid on concentration for other things - steals time - is a sin - makes me nervous, bad for my health, preoccupies my every thought process

First John 3:8 tells us that Jesus came "to destroy the devil's work." Jesus came to get back for us all that the enemy was allowed to take through Adam and Eve's rebellion. Satan tries to get us to think of worry as a truly caring attitude, so we won't realize the damage it does in our lives.

When one of our children was sick for a few days, a neighbor called to express her concern. She said, "Tell David I'm so sorry he's sick. I worried about him all night." She felt her all-night worrying would show us how much she cared.

When a dog chews aggressively on a bone, an old-fashioned expression describes the dog as "worrying that bone." When our minds "chew" at a subject, we "worry" that subject, and Satan uses our fretting to steal, kill and destroy, no matter how much we may try to justify our behavior.

When you find yourself spending a lot of mind time "chewing" on some subject, check to see if your thoughts are adding to your peace of mind or stealing from it.

Can you tell when you are worried? How does it affect you?

Makes me unable to do my best - steals my joy of the present.

How does your worrying affect others around you?

Keeps me from the moment and cheats them of our time together.

XX

What are some of the reasons you use to justify your worry?

I don't any more. I still fall back
but when I realize I am doing it
I try to focus on Jesus and deter
Satan.

Do you remember how Jesus said to Martha, "Martha, Martha . . . you are worried and upset about many things" (Luke 10:41)? Read John 11:5 to find out Jesus' motive for addressing this problem in her life. Now refer back to John 10:10. Why does Jesus want us to be free from worry in our lives?

So he can live life to the fullest
without thinking about the past
or the future.

Read Mark 2:1-12. Notice how much the paralyzed man's four friends cared about his situation. They went to tremendous effort to bring their friend to Jesus, but after they lowered their friend through the roof, they left the situation in the hands of Jesus. They didn't tell Jesus what to do or even suggest what the man needed. They brought him to the One who could make a difference and trusted Him to do what was best. Mark wrote, "When Jesus saw their faith, he said to the paralytic, 'Son, your sins are forgiven'" (verse 5).

I don't know about you, but I would have felt compelled to speak up and say, "Please, Jesus, we want You to heal him, so he can walk."

However, the man's friends kept quiet and waited, trusting the wisdom of the One to whom they had brought their friend.

Then, after addressing the teachers of the law concerning their sinful attitudes, Jesus spoke again to the paralytic, "I tell you, get up, take your mat and go home" (verse 11).

In this instance, Jesus knew it was necessary to deal with the paralytic man's spiritual need before addressing his physical need.

There is within the attitude of worry the pressing need to solve the problem now, to relieve the stress of the situation, to take control so that the desired results will come to pass. True compassion throbs with the need to bring the problem to the One who knows what is best and can be trusted to bring godly good out of the need. God alone knows how to bring real deliverance.

What problems are you trying to solve with your own reasoning? How many "paralytics" are you struggling to help walk when they need to be brought on the "mat of faith" to Jesus?

My strength and lack of understanding certain situations, trying to get our family to know Jesus w/o hitting them on the head with it.

A Bible study teacher explained, "When a problem comes, I take it immediately to God. If I don't have the strength to take it there myself and leave it, I get two or three friends to pray with me until I know the situation is safely in God's hands. Then we wait to see what God will do or what He might tell us to do."

Worry makes the worrier feel as if *he* or *she* is the center of the situation and overly responsible for its solution. Godly compassion makes *God* the center and the One responsible for directing what needs to be done . . . or left undone!

A Closer Look at My Own Heart

Because Jesus loves us and gave Himself to set us free from the works of the devil, He is always ready to help us identify and refuse the worry that tries to invade our thinking. He doesn't want us to be burdened with the kind of problems and responsibilities that worry presses upon us. Jesus said, "My yoke is easy and my burden is light" (Matthew 11:30).

The burdens of worry are heavy and generated most often by an unreasonable fear. One of the best definitions that I have found says worry is "a cycle of unproductive thoughts whirling around a center of hidden fear." The whirling, unproductive thoughts will be full of the what-ifs and maybes that contribute to the lack of truth in our thinking. Most often, the truth we don't want to admit is that our worry, seemingly so caring, is really centered in a self-protective fear of some kind.

Beverly asked our Bible study to pray that her son, Ted, a high-school senior, would pass his chemistry regents. The urgency of her request mirrored her fear of his failure.

We asked Bev about the importance of his passing. She explained, "If he fails, he'll have to retake the course and probably won't get into college in the fall."

Probing a little more, I asked, "Why is that so bad? Is it important he go to college in the fall?"

Bev replied, "But if he fails, it will look like he didn't study, that we weren't responsible as parents. I guess it means I'll feel ashamed before the other parents that my son didn't measure up."

"What's your bottom-line prayer for Ted, Bev?" I asked.

After a moment's hesitation, she answered, "For Ted to know Jesus Christ in a personal way."

"What if part of God's plan for Ted to see his need of Jesus is for Ted to fail his chemistry regents? How would you feel about that?" I asked.

"I see what you mean," she replied. "I'm ready to pray now." She led us in a prayer for her son, asking God to do with both Ted and the chemistry regents what He knew was best for Ted's salvation. When she finished, Bev said, "I feel better now. The anxiety is gone, and I know God will take care of the outcome in the way that's best."

How many of our worries whirl around the fear of some embarrassment coming to us through our own actions or the actions of those who are connected to us in some way? Identify such a fear in your collection of worried thoughts. How does this fear affect your thought life?

Dick not taking all his pills. I think I should be responsible for cke & his taking them. Always reminding him & it drives him & me

How does this fear affect your actions?

for - makes me take my time to keep him focused

First Peter 5:5 says, "God opposes the proud but gives grace to the humble." The succeeding verses continue by saying, "Humble yourselves, therefore, under God's mighty hand, that he may lift you up in due time. Cast all your anxiety on him because he cares for you" (1 Peter 5:6-7).

Think about why it's so hard to give *all* our anxieties over to God. Could it be because we don't trust God to make things turn out the way *we* want them to turn out? Is it because He seems so slow in answering? Or do we believe the false idea that God isn't interested in our small prob-lems—that we should be able to work those out for ourselves—and expects us to ask for His help only with big things?

Why do you hesitate to give God *all* your cares?

They seem so petty & I should be able
to figure it out w/o bothering him.

Peter warned believers, "Be self-controlled and alert. Your enemy the devil prowls around like a roaring lion looking for someone to devour" (1 Peter 5:8). As in the Garden with Adam and Eve, Satan prowls around in the gar-dens of our lives, trying to get us to deny God and His loving care for us.

Identify a situation where fear and pride have combined to make you feel eaten up with worry.

When I am with people who I think don't care
for me and I need to be with them. I do
pray before I go but my pride is keeping me
from letting God do his work.

When we identify a worry place where Satan is prowling, Peter com-manded, "Resist him, standing firm in the faith" (1 Peter 5:9). As we learn to identify worry for what it is, then we can begin to learn the way to resist Satan's attacks on our lives.

Action Steps I Can Take Today

It becomes necessary in any spiritual battle to find and face the truth about our weaknesses. If we label fear and worry for what they are, we have taken a big step toward lessening their power over us.

Write your own definition of worry, using the things you have learned from this lesson and from your own personal experience.

Worry/fear is a Thief, of time, joy, love,
success, stagnation, — I label it and
destroy Satan attempt to control us & keep
from from God.

Ps 55   Donna

Go through the list of worries that you made in chapter 1 and ask God to show you the fear that is at the center of each one. If you have difficulty in identifying each fear, just leave it for now and trust God to show you at a later time.

As you identify each fear, pray about each worry: "Father, I'm worried about this because I am afraid of _____. I want to trust You to take care of this situation. Please help me. In Jesus' name, amen."

⤳ ✛ ⤶

While teaching a Bible study on another topic, I mentioned that worry is sin and needs to be dealt with in our lives. Later a young woman approached me and declared vehemently, "Worry can't be sin. If it is, I've been sinning all my life." She left and never returned to the study.

Is worry a sin? Now that we've distinguished between worry and compassion, anxiety and concern, in the next chapter we'll look at what Scripture says worry is. Can it really be a sin since everybody does it? What does God say?

THREE

𝒞ALLING A SIN A SIN

*Choosing to be free from worry brings us face to face with
the importance of recognizing worry as sin.*

One man, ever looking for the practical way to deal with a problem, said, "I was glad when I finally saw worry as sin. Then I could do with it as I would any sin—first confession, then forgiveness and finally God's help to overcome."

Facing God's truth about any sin in our lives costs us a struggle. But facing the truth about worry seems to present a bigger challenge than some other sins—perhaps because worry is so common a transgression. As one young Christian person put it, "How can worry be a sin? Everybody I know does it."

It is hard to go against the crowd. But the kingdom of God is not a democracy where the majority rules. God's kingdom has just one standard—His.

Before working through this chapter, pray: "Father, help me to call worry what You call it. Amen."

A Closer Look at the Problem

Worry exercises a great deal of influence in the lives of Christians and therefore in the Church itself, because we fail to recognize it as a sin against God. Let's eavesdrop on a conversation.

Edward: Lord, I don't know what to do. My wife is sick, the kids are sick, and it looks like I might lose my job. How will I pay the doctor bills and the mortgage and the car payment and buy food if I don't have a job? You have to do something, Lord. I can't stand all this pressure.

God: Edward, are you worried?

> *Edward:*   Of course! There're so many problems. What if I can't handle them all? I just don't know what I'll do if I'm laid off.
> *God:*   Edward, are you worried?
> *Edward:* Yes, Lord, I guess I am. But . . .
> *God:*   Edward, when I worry, *then* you can worry.

Does God worry? Jesus illustrated God's compassion, but He never in any way showed God as anxious or fretting about difficult people or situations in the world. God is not a worrier, and He doesn't want those who belong to Him to be worriers either.

A Closer Look at God's Truth

Hebrews 1:2-3 tells us that in these last days, God has spoken to us through His Son, who is "the express image of His person" (*NKJV*). We'll begin by looking at what Jesus told us about worry.

Read Matthew 6:25-34. About what things did Jesus tell us *not* to worry?

God tells us he will take care of all our needs. Worry steals our time and accomplishes nothing. Be happy with the moment and live.

Why do you think Jesus listed these particular things?

So we learn to trust him and depend on him for everything and follow his examples.

To what does God compare our value?

Birds flowers, grass. Showing us just how well he takes care of them and he considers us more valuable than they.

Read Genesis 1:26-27 to discover why we human beings are of more value than the birds or the lilies. God's desire has always been that we not only be made in His image but also that we have His character. Is there fear or worry anywhere in the nature of God or His Son, Jesus?

What challenging question did Jesus ask in Matthew 6:27?

Who of you by worring can add a single hour to his life?

Do you think worry adds to the quality or length of your life? One woman explained, "The things I worry about never happen, so I see worry as kind of a preventative." What do you think of her reasoning?

Totaling opposite of what it does. Worring increases your stress which shortens your life — I ck medical records. Trust God and live longer.

What is your reaction to the claims of some in the medical profession that worry may actually shorten our life span?

I've seen it happen. Bobby, my Dad.

How does worrying relate to Satan's attempt to kill, steal and destroy in our lives?

Satan does whatever he can to separate us from the Lord. We know that worry is a sin so it works in his plan.

The command of Jesus concerning worry comes from His love for us. He speaks to us about worry as we might speak to a friend reaching for a poisonous drink: "Stop! Don't touch that!" If Jesus says "do not" and we do, have we been disobedient? Why or why not?

Yes we have been disobedient because he told us he will take care of us always. He has the plan

What word does God use to describe disobedience to His Word? What, then, does that make worry?

It is sin.

Jesus never gave us a "do not" without giving a positive direction for us to take instead of the forbidden one. According to Matthew 6:33, what did Jesus tell us to seek *first*? What did He promise will follow our seeking God's way first?

Seek 1st the kingdom of heaven and his righteousness and all things will be given to you as well.

If I drop a dangling mobile (like we hang over a baby's crib) on the floor, how would you pick it up? Would you grab the first string you saw or would you hunt for the center hook? If you picked the mobile up by the string nearest you, what would be the result?

It could break and disconnect form the center hook.

Taking time to find the center of the mobile means all the attached pieces will fall into place as you lift it up. Jesus told us that the way to deal with our problems is to seek God first, recognizing Him as the center. Then our difficulties will fall into a manageable order, and we will know how to think and what to do about the things causing us anxiety.

In Matthew 6:34, Jesus told us not to worry about tomorrow. He didn't mean we are not to think about tomorrow or make future plans, but the *motivation* for our planning is not to be anxiety. In these days, why does it seem unrealistic not to worry about the future?

Health, financial situation, loved ones — destiny on earth.

If worry about tomorrow was a sin in Jesus' time, is it still a sin today? Why?

God asked we love +trust Him with all our heart, mind + being. Worry is a sign we do not trust He will take care of us.

Remember that "Jesus Christ is the same yesterday and today and forever" (Hebrews 13:8). People of His day could be free from worry, if they chose to trust God to make them able. Followers of God today have that same privilege and responsibility. If it is true that we have more cause to worry than the people of Jesus' day, God will be faithful to provide more grace for us. God never asks us to obey a command without giving us what we need to be obedient.

A Closer Look at My Own Heart

Think about these words: "May the words of my mouth and the meditation of my heart be pleasing in your sight, O Lord, my Rock and my Redeemer" (Psalm 19:14).

When our hearts are full of worry and our heads full of unproductive thoughts whirling around a center of hidden fear, are our meditations acceptable in the sight of One who said, "Do not worry"? Why or why not?

Worry is the time stealer. Use that time to pray about your concerns and move on with today's needs.

Remember that Jesus also said, "For out of the overflow of the heart the mouth speaks" (Matthew 12:34). What kind of words will result from our worry-filled heart?

Anger, fear, mistrust, unkind remarks, grieve.

What kind of words do you hear spoken by worried people?

Swearing, threats, misguided remarks, and hopeless thinking.

How does worry affect *your* conversation?

Negative, fearful, unstable and sadness.

Psalm 37 has much to say about the fretting that accompanies our worry. Verses 1 and 7 warn us not to fret about evildoers or those who prosper because of evil schemes. In our world today, human reasoning would tell us that we have to be upset and worried about the increase of evil and the success of those who scheme to prosper by deception. But remember the words of Proverbs 3:5: "Trust in the LORD with all your heart and lean not on your own understanding."

Are you willing to give up your fretting about the unwelcome events in your life? How about your fretting about evil situations and deceptive leaders—even if it does make such stimulating coffee talk?

I guess I never thought about the world situation showing up as worry. But I will work on trying not to get worked up and maybe do more to try and find positive.

How would your meditations and conversations change if you began to focus more on the realities of God's kingdom and less on the uncertainties of man's world?

I think when you are conversing about world situations that is one thing. When we talk about them and each person trys to find some positive way to improve it will do. If not we need to take it to God.

Psalm 37:8 says, "Cease from anger, and forsake wrath; do not fret—it only causes harm" (*NKJV*). In your own life, what harm has been caused by worry-induced anger and fretting?

Separation instead of uniting to try to find a solution and if it is beyond our realm of help than turn it over to God.

It is difficult for us to accept the fact that it's more important not to sin against God by worrying than it is to get our problem solved. We reason, *If God will just take care of this problem, then I won't sin because I won't have anything to worry about.* Yet God wants us to give up our worry—because it separates us from Him and causes harm to us—even if our problem is never resolved. He knows the sin of worry will do us more harm than the problem, though we may not be able to see the danger. Also, He knows a worry-induced solution will only bring more distress in the end. So He urges us to come to Him *first*. The psalmist wrote:

Trust in the LORD, and do good;
Dwell in the land, and feed on His faithfulness.

Delight yourself also in the LORD,
And He shall give you the desires of your heart
(Psalm 37:3-4, *NKJV*).

When we read these words, we hear God urging us to "feed" on the evidences of His faithfulness rather than the threats of our difficulty.

When a problem arises, do we trust God enough to turn *first* to prayer, then read His Word and then recall His past faithfulness? Or do we set our mind immediately on seeking solutions for the problem?

As honestly as you can, describe the fears that keep you from trusting God and that keep you centering on your problems rather than on God's faithfulness.

Loss of independency. Most times it is a short worry (as thanks to this book I am grounded quickly to God. Gone until the next injury or just aging thing shows up and it repeats itself.

What does verse 4 of Psalm 37 say will happen? Do you believe your fears or your heavenly Father?

Delight yourself in the Lord & he will give you the desires of your heart. I believe the father. I wish I could not be reminded so much by TV, people, my body about aging because really that is the reason I think about mostly these days.

Psalm 37 tells us to turn our heart meditations toward God in spite of all that seems wrong around us. The words of Jesus to Martha encouraged her to come to Him *first*, before she tackled all the things that had her worried and troubled. In Matthew 6:25, Jesus commanded, "Do not worry," and then He commanded, "Seek *first* [God's] kingdom" (Matthew 6:33, emphasis added). The only way to be free from worry in our lives is for us to recognize worry as a sin that draws our focus away from God. Once we call worry a sin, we've already begun to break its hold in our lives. Jesus promised to those who would hold to His teaching, "You will know the truth, and the truth will set you free" (John 8:32).

Action Steps I Can Take Today

We understand sin as rebellion against God. We acknowledge that the worry in our lives contradicts the many biblical admonitions to turn from our anxious thoughts and meditate on God's faithfulness. We can say with our mouths that worry is sin, but how will we begin to work out the confession, repentance and changed thinking needed to overcome this sin in our lives?

Write down one of your most pressing worries. Now determine how this worry is rebellion against God. If you're not sure, pray and ask God to help you see the worry as He does.

Lack of self discipline these days — seems like I eat things I know I should not and drink more wine than I want, which both lead to overweight I do not want. Why — Where is my self control? I pray & as soon as I am tested I fail. Why?

Just as soon as you find yourself worrying, confess your specific worry to God and ask forgiveness: "Lord, I'm worried about Johnny's cough; I'm afraid he's getting sick. Please forgive me and help me to trust You." It may seem you're confessing and asking forgiveness over and over at first, but just the fact you're recognizing the need to confess and ask forgiveness is saying to the enemy that you are no longer deceived about the worry in your life. Agreeing with God and asking for His help is a major step in your walk.

Memorize the command and promise of Matthew 6:33: "Seek first the kingdom of God and His righteousness, and all these things shall be added to you" (NKJV). Put it in the meditation file of your heart.

Begin to pray for someone you know who struggles with worry. Do this without condemnation or judgment. It is a way for you to begin to freely give what God is giving you: the way out of worry's bondage.

⚜

Lorrie's argument sounded good. "Look," she said, "my mother was a worrier and my grandmother before her. You don't really think I can break this pattern in my life, do you? I wouldn't know how to respond to life if I didn't worry."

Who *is* in charge of the way we think? Is it our parents, our grandparents, the media or the crowd? It's a question we'll consider in the next chapter as we discover how God will enable us to carry out our choices.

FOUR

$\mathscr{M}$AKING YOUR VOTE COUNT

Have you ever laughed at an enthusiastic puppy whose ever-moving tail seemed to wag him, propelling him along in spite of himself? In the same way, anxiety's ever-pushing fears may cause worry to propel us along, seemingly in spite of ourselves—and it's no laughing matter.

When my friend makes a trip to visit her sister, she must change planes at a large airport. My friend has a fear of losing her way, of missing her flight, of not being able to manage alone the possible problems such a change involves. So out of fear she is deciding that it might be better to take the train, even though it would add another travel day. Or maybe a friend could go with her for the three weeks, even though the friend's presence would change the whole chemistry of the visit with her sister. Can you see how anxiety is becoming a control factor in her life?

When problems press in on every side, it is hard to believe God doesn't expect us to worry. It seems as impossible for us to stop the worried thoughts as it is for an enthusiastic puppy to keep his tail still. Yet when the psalmist describes a time of extreme turmoil in Psalm 46:10, in the midst of it all the Lord commands, "Be still, and know that I am God."

God's Word makes it clear that His people have a choice. No work of the enemy, no problem of our own making, no natural disaster can *make* us worry. We *choose* to worry, even though it feels as if we can't help it. Remember the three votes? In every situation of our lives, three votes are cast. God always votes for us; Satan always votes against us. Who has the deciding vote? We do. By giving us such a choice, God has put us in charge of whether or not we worry.

Now would be a good time to pray: "Lord, make me aware when I choose to worry and show me how to vote against worry's control in my life. Amen."

A Closer Look at the Problem

Satan tries to make us think we have no choice. He tells us, "It's only human to worry; you can't help it." Have you ever agreed with him, saying, "Sure I worry. After all, I'm only human"?

The enemy speaks his usual partial truth. Fear and worry are part of our human inheritance from Adam and Eve. However, if we have received Jesus Christ as Savior and Lord, we are never again "only human." We are empowered by Christ's life within us to overcome the worry that invades our lives. As God-indwelt vessels, we are meant to be in charge of loosing God's power against the sin waves of worry.

Isaiah 12:2 says:

> Surely God is my salvation;
> I will trust and not be afraid.
> The LORD, the LORD, is my strength and my song;
> he has become my salvation.

What does the writer affirm in the first line? What does this tell us about God's vote?

_____

_____

_____

_____

_____

What does the second line say about the writer's vote? Upon what is his vote based?

_____

_____

_____

_____

The one speaking these words in Isaiah has made a decision. God *is* his salvation; this is truth. He decides he will trust this truth and not be afraid, and he affirms that the strength he needs and the joy he will experience come out of his relationship with his God. As he believes and acts on that truth by faith, God *becomes* his salvation in actual experience.

As Christians, we decide whether worry or trust will rule in our lives. God says, "Trust." Satan says, "Worry." When we choose to say, "I will trust and not worry," the God who is our salvation will manifest Himself.

Fill in lines 1 and 4 of Isaiah 12:2:

Surely God _____ my salvation;
He _____ my salvation.

Between the two statements, there is the all-important declaration of the speaker's trust, a declaration that indicates believing actions will follow believing words. How do our actions prove our words?

_____
_____
_____

A man has a rope ladder to drop out his bedroom window in case of fire. He often looks at the rope, comforted by the thought that it *is* his way of escape—his salvation—in case of fire. One night a fire occurs. The man grabs the rope ladder and hurriedly hangs it out the window. The flimsy ladder looks inadequate, but the man chooses to trust it and not be afraid. Down the ladder he goes to safety. The man's actions prove his trust, and the ladder *becomes* his salvation from the fire.

In the same way, God is always available for our salvation from worry. He literally becomes that salvation when worry attacks us and we choose to trust Him. Just as the man was in charge of deciding to use the rope ladder for his escape, we are in charge of deciding to draw upon God's power to be free from worry.

"I know I shouldn't worry, but I just can't seem to help it." How many times do we say these words as we struggle to get victory over anxiety? Now we are learning that we are responsible for "helping it," but how? From where do we get the ability to take charge when worry attacks?

A Closer Look at God's Truth

God never gives His people a command they cannot follow if they are willing to trust and obey His instructions. For us to be obedient to God's instructions, we need more than a human willingness to try.

In his letter to the Colossians, Paul wrote of the mystery that has been revealed to the saints—those who have placed their faith in Jesus Christ: "To [the saints] God has chosen to make known among the Gentiles the glorious riches of this mystery, which is Christ in you, the hope of glory" (Colossians 1:27). What does this verse tell us about our being much more than *only human*?

_____

_____

_____

_____

God doesn't ask us to stand against worry in our human strength. He knows we can't. Jesus Himself said, "Apart from me you can do nothing" (John 15:5). But when we become a Christian, we then have the Spirit of Jesus living in us to stand against anxiety's attacks. Because of this mystery, we can look for God's glory to be revealed within the problem, not just in its solution.

We're often heard whining, "But Jesus doesn't know what it's like for me. He was never in my situation." The sin of worry isn't related to any particular situation; it's related to our particular reaction in any situation.

When a problem comes (no matter its size or severity), do you react out of your human nature, or do you respond out of the Christ-life within you?

_____

_____

_____

_____

Read Hebrews 4:14-15. Did Jesus ever face worry temptations like we do? The Bible says Jesus was tempted in every way, just as we are. There's no note in the margin saying "except for worry." So if Jesus was tempted to worry, just like we are, and "yet was without sin" (verse 15), what does that tell us about the worry-resisting ability of His life in us?

_____

_____

_____

_____

Now read Hebrews 2:17-18. The writer explained how "in every way" Jesus had to be made like us in order to face and defeat all the temptations and destructions Satan brings against us. According to verse 18, how easy was it for Jesus to face the temptations (including the temptation to worry) without giving in to sin?

_____

_____

_____

_____

The closing words of verse 18 encourage us as we face our temptations: "He is able to help those who are being tempted." How do these words fit with Paul's description of the "mystery" we can have within us?

_____

_____

_____

_____

Christ faced the temptation to worry when He lived on earth, for He was tempted in every way we are. Yet He stood against the temptation, suffering the struggle of worry versus trust, winning over the enemy's attempts to defeat Him. Perhaps at 12 or 16 or even 20 years of age, Jesus was tempted to worry about how and when He was ever going to get on the road and go about His Father's business. Perhaps at age 30, coming out of the calm of the carpenter shop, He was tempted to worry about how He would find time to be alone with the Father or time to rest before the next onslaught of the crowds.

We know Jesus suffered in the garden, facing the agony of the Cross. Was He tempted to worry about His ability to do what the Father wanted—could He go through with it? And what about on the Cross? Could Jesus have been tempted to worry about whether it was all going to turn out like the Father had told Him it would? This dying for the sins of others had never been done before and all Jesus had to depend on was His Father's word. Would He really raise Him from the dead? It's important to remember that Jesus walked the earth with the same trust challenge we face—depending only on His Father's Word and His Father's salvation in every situation.

We know Jesus didn't give in to the sin of anxiety. He won the victory not only for Himself but also for us. In every battle, He voted with the

Father and against the enemy. So now His Spirit lives in us to enable us to vote with the Father, to empower us to resist the sin of worry. If we choose to trust, He will enable.

A Closer Look at My Own Heart

You, like many others, may have been reading along in this study without evaluating your own personal relationship with Jesus Christ. Since it's impossible for a person to break worry's bondage unless he or she has the Spirit of Christ living in him or her, you may want to make sure His Spirit *does* live in you.

Romans 8:9 says, "You are not in the flesh but in the Spirit, if indeed the Spirit of God dwells in you. Now if anyone does not have the Spirit of Christ, he is not His" (*NKJV*). Do you know that Christ's Spirit lives in you today? If you've never experienced a personal relationship with Jesus Christ or question whether you have, the following prayer, offered from an honest and seeking heart, will bring you into the kingdom of God, and it will bring the Spirit of the living Christ to dwell in you. If you have never prayed to receive the Spirit of Christ within you, this is the first step in your choosing to be in charge. Pray aloud:

> *God, I can't deal with sin in my life. I need a Savior, and right now I ask Your Son, Jesus, to become my Savior and Lord. I ask forgiveness for all my sins, and I receive the Spirit of Jesus Christ to live in me. Thank You for answering my prayer and making me a child of Your kingdom. In Jesus' name, amen.*

How do we now begin to exercise our Christ-given ability to be in charge of our worry? In Philippians 4:11-13, Paul uses a word that explains how we discover that biblical truth will work in real life: "For I have *learned* to be content whatever the circumstances. I know what it is to be in need, and I know what it is to have plenty. I have *learned* the secret of being content in any and every situation" (emphasis added). To have this kind of contentment requires truly overcoming fear and anxiety.

How do you suppose Paul had arrived at this place in his life?

_____

_____

_____

What does the use of the word "learned" imply about the process involved in coming to trust the power of the life of Christ in us?

_____

_____

_____

_____

In Philippians 4:13, how did Paul explain his ability to be content?

_____

_____

_____

Once again we see that the power to resist worry isn't determined by the situations in our lives but rather by our trust in the One who defeated the sin of worry and who now lives in us to carry out His victory in our personal problems.

What is the state of your heart right now? Are you willing to learn (even if it seems impossible) how to take charge of the worry temptations that draw you into sin?

_____

_____

_____

_____

Action Steps I Can Take Today

One of the best preparations we can make for becoming free from worry is memorizing Scripture verses to use against the worry waves when they threaten to overwhelm us.

Memorize Isaiah 26:3: "You will keep in perfect peace him whose mind is steadfast, because he trusts in you." The *New King James Version* is translated this way: "You will keep him in perfect peace, whose mind is stayed on You, because he trusts in You."

After you have learned the verse, practice making it personal: "Lord, thank You that You keep me in perfect peace as I keep my mind on You instead of on the problem, because I choose to trust You."

Meditate on 1 Corinthians 10:13: "No temptation has seized you except what is common to man. And God is faithful; he will not let you be tempted beyond what you can bear. But when you are tempted, he will also provide a way out so that you can stand up under it." Consider the following points:

- How does it make you feel to know your worries are common to other people? Has the enemy tried to make you think, *No one ever had the problems I do?*

- Since God won't allow you to be tempted beyond what you're able to resist, what does that say about your ability to resist the worry in your life?

- Since God has promised to make a way of escape—from the worry, not necessarily from the problem—are you willing to ask Him for help and then do whatever He shows you? What would make you hesitate?

Sometimes I find it necessary to pray, "Please, Lord, show me the way of escape from this temptation to worry—and make me willing to do what you show me." There are times when it looks easier to give in and worry than to take the way of escape.

Share a personal testimony with someone, telling them what you are learning about worry. Don't try to convince them that they need to change; just share! And continue to pray for the person you chose to pray for in the last session.

As Kathy looked over the *Free from Worry* book, she commented, "Somebody would have to give me a whole new mind for me to give up worrying. That's just the way my thoughts go. In fact, I don't know what I'd think about if I didn't worry."

Many of us understand Kathy's comment. Our minds are programmed to meet each situation with the "what ifs" and "maybes" of the worry program we've developed over the years. In chapter 5, we'll explore the reality of developing a new mind—one that responds to people and things with the thoughts of God rather than the thoughts of only-human reasoning.

Having a New Mind

"I wish I could shut off my mind," complained Mary. "The same upsetting thoughts just keep going around and around. When I fall asleep I get a break, but as soon as I wake up, the thoughts are right there waiting for me."

Mary's description of her thought life fits the definition of "worry" we talked about in chapter 2: "a cycle of unproductive thoughts whirling around a center of hidden fear." It becomes apparent that a major step for us to become free from worry must be the changing of our mind habits. We know how difficult it can be to break a habit, especially if it has become established over a lifetime of living. But we can take comfort from Paul's words: "I can do everything through him who gives me strength" (Philippians 4:13).

As we begin this chapter, let's pray: "Lord, I don't understand how I can have a mind free from worry, but I trust You to teach me. Show me Your way of escape from the temptation to dwell on worry thoughts, and make me able to do what You show me. Amen."

A Closer Look at the Problem

We have established that worry is sin. But before actual sin takes place, there comes temptation. Strong temptations to worry come at us daily. A new pain in our body, a troubling phone call, a mistake in our checkbook or even a five-minute summary of the world news can create fertile soil where seeds of worry take root.

Have you noticed how media advertising feeds our worries just to get us to buy a product? There used to be a deodorant ad that raised the question, "Are you *sure*?" That challenging approach was designed to generate an uncertainty about body odor: Did you give off an offensive smell? Then, to take care of the worry the ad had created, the consumer was urged to use the only safe deodorant, which happened to be called "Sure."

However, changing our worry patterns isn't as simple as changing our deodorant. When we have entrenched worry patterns in our mind, as soon as one problem is solved, we will find another to feed our worried thoughts.

One day I decided to "fix" all my neighbor's worries. I took care of each thing she found disturbing and brought her each item she fretted about not having in her cupboard. When the list was complete, I said, "There. Now we've taken care of everything that was bothering you. Don't you feel relieved?"

She looked at me a moment and then said with a worried expression, "I wonder what I forgot."

No matter how many problems I solved for my neighbor, I could never set her free from the worry in her life. Only the work of Jesus Christ and His life in her (or in us!) can accomplish such deliverance.

Hebrews 2:18 in the *New English Bible* says, "For since he himself has passed through the test of suffering, he is able to help those who are meeting their test now." *The Living Bible* paraphrases the verse: "For since he himself has now been through suffering and temptation, he knows what it is like when we suffer and are tempted, and he is wonderfully able to help us." Jesus resisted worry and refused to let it draw Him into sin.

What does this verse tell us about the difficulty of Jesus' struggle and of His ability to help us now?

Jesus knows what it is like to suffer. Jesus example of resisted worry + not let it drawn him into sin. Follow example,

This verse is often overlooked by those who think Jesus' life was easy because He was the Son of God. We hear the reasoning, "But He was Jesus; I'm just a human being." Philippians 2:6-7 explains, "[Jesus], being in very nature God, did not consider equality with God something to be grasped, but made himself nothing, taking the very nature of a servant, being made in human likeness."

We tend to think of Jesus as a kind of Superman. The fictional Superman was a powerful, other-worldly being who disguised himself as the human reporter Clark Kent. When trouble came, Clark would disappear into a phone booth, strip off his disguise and reappear sporting a big *S* on his chest, revealing his true identity. Superman only pretended to be human and resorted to the use of his extraordinary powers whenever they were needed.

Jesus, however, laid aside the omnipotent attributes that would have marked Him as other-worldly. When confronted with a challenge, Jesus didn't discard His carpenter's robe and come to the rescue with a big G on His chest. Although He was God, Jesus became a man, deliberately confining Himself to a human body. He drew only upon the power of the Holy Spirit that was within Him from birth—the same Holy Spirit who comes to live in us when we invite Jesus Christ to be our Lord and Savior.

Jesus was not God dressed up like a man; He *became* a man. He humbled Himself and became totally dependent upon His Father's guidance and empowerment to live as the Son of Man among men.

We see this illustrated when Jesus said to Peter in the garden, "Do you think I cannot call on my Father, and he will at once put at my disposal more than twelve legions of angels? But how then would the Scriptures be fulfilled that say it must happen in this way?" (Matthew 26:53-54). Jesus' death and resurrection were foretold throughout Old Testament Scriptures. Jesus wouldn't try to escape His Father's plan by drawing on power He had willingly laid aside when He took on human form. Jesus chose to do as His Father desired, trusting His Father to give Him the strength He needed.

Jesus had laid aside what we would call his "Superman" powers and refused to pick them up to save Himself from the cross. He experienced the agony of the crucifixion in human flesh, strengthened by the Holy Spirit within. Taking upon Himself the pain and penalty of our sin, Jesus provided for all mankind the way of escape from Satan's entrapment. Never forget that Jesus Christ experienced in His flesh all the temptations of our agonies, our desperations, our worries. Then He died to set us free from them.

Our flesh nature will struggle and protest when we choose to travel God's path instead of humanity's way. This same struggle had to occur and be overcome in the life of Jesus for Him to identify with us and help us in our battle against sin.

Read Hebrews 5:7-10. How does verse 7 show us the humanity of Jesus as He cried out to the Father?

We are weak & need him to help us to understand and give strength to keep us focused on him & his desires for us to life

The times of loud cries and tears didn't occur just during Jesus' wilderness temptation or in the garden before His crucifixion but during *all* "the days of Jesus' life on earth." As we are instructed to do, Jesus cried out to His Father, asking to be shown the way of escape, so He would not sin.

Hebrews 5:8 tells us that "although he was a son, he learned obedience from what he suffered." So often we have the misconception that Jesus came preprogrammed to obey. We think obedience was automatic for Him because He was God.

But living in a human body made Jesus subject to all the temptations of the flesh, just as we are. Although the Spirit within Him was willing, Jesus' flesh had to be disciplined to yield to the will of God. As the Spirit-filled, Spirit-led Son of Man, Jesus learned how, through obedience, to keep the temptations of His human flesh from drawing Him into sin.

Jesus learned, Paul learned, and we will need to learn, too, that a transformed mind—one that will know how to resist worry and find strength in God thoughts—will not come without a struggle. We will experience temptations and tears, but if we keep our face turned toward God, He will bring us through by the power of His Son who dwells in us.

Jesus said we are to count the cost of following Him (see Luke 14:25-45). How much effort are you willing to put forth in order to be free of worry's control in your life—to obey the command of Jesus, "Do not worry"?

As much as is needed. I try & sometimes I do make it work & sometimes I fail. I put my best effort & ask Jesus to help especially when I feel like I am failing

A Closer Look at God's Truth

For us to have the courage to be free from worry, we need to understand what happened at the Cross. Remembering that worry is sin, let's consider what Jesus accomplished concerning sin at Calvary.

God knew we couldn't save ourselves from sin or from the death penalty that accompanies it. So God did the impossible for us by sending His Son in human flesh. Born of the Spirit (rather than of Adam's seed) but living in a fleshly body, Jesus battled to consistently choose the way of the Spirit over the flesh and became the sinless, perfect sacrifice needed for man's redemption. The power of *all* sin was broken forever; the requirements of its death penalty were paid at the cross. Jesus made salvation available to anyone who would choose the way of escape He provided.

Read Romans 8:1-9. The salvation Jesus provided becomes a reality only to those who have made Jesus their Savior and Lord. According to verse 5, how does the person who has chosen Jesus' way of salvation live?

A life of peace

What does it mean to "set" your mind on something?

Stay focused and make it happen through determination & work.

Why is this setting of the mind important in order to be free from worry?

You must put all into becoming free according to God rules.

Contrast life according to the Spirit with life according to the sinful nature as described in verses 6-8. Where does a mind set on fear and worry fit in this description?

Leads to death.

According to verse 9, how are we as Christians to be controlled? How is this possible?

The spirit of God lives in us all who believe.

First Corinthians 2:16 offers a marvelous truth to those who know Jesus
Christ as Lord and Savior. At the moment we receive the life of Christ in
us, what do we also receive?

We have the mind of Christ.

Jesus knows worry is powerless to keep us in bondage because He defeated
it. His mind, which knows the way to freedom, is in us. He will, if we trust
Him, not only show us how to think about worry temptations, but will
also show us how to escape them. Read Romans 12:1-2. What are the two
things Paul urges us to do?

*Be transformed by renewing your mind
and you will be able to know Gods
will. God wants us to be good + pleasing
to him.*

Why do you think these two things are important in order for us to be free
from worry?

*Work on what God wants from us
by focusing + studying his work and
do good because of it and trust him.*

If our bodies are truly presented to God for Him to use as He wills, so
much of what we worry about loses its importance. What we will eat, what
we will wear, what will happen to our physical bodies become God's responsibility, not ours. Now, that doesn't mean we no longer have to go
grocery shopping or care about how we dress, but if we are entrusting ourselves to God, we can trust Him to direct us, even in these seemingly mun-
dane things. Many times I find myself praying over the meat counter or
when shopping for clothes. Does God care about these small things? Of
course He does. If my body is yielded to Him, He cares about what I put in
and on it. My part is to trust both His interest and His direction.

In Romans 12:2, what does Paul tell us not to do? How are we to begin to change in our conformity to the world?

Have clean thoughts + action and continue to follow him and be good faithful + [illegible]

What are some ways a change in your thinking would affect your actions? For example, how would your actions be affected if you practiced Jesus' instruction to "love your enemies, bless those who curse you, do good to those who hate you, and pray for those who spitefully use you and persecute you" (Matthew 5:44, *NKJV*)?

I would find peace and by praying it is the answer to showing love!

If you practiced this, believing it was best because it is God's way, what would happen to your fretting about past hurts, worrying about running into that person who doesn't like you, and so forth? (Remember, the question isn't whether or not we *can* change our thought patterns but *will* we.)

I will give us a peace of comfort knowing that we turned it to our Lord & he will take care of it and we can go into something we can do on earth + within our capabilities

At the end of verse 2 in the Romans 12 passage, Paul tells us that the presentation of our bodies and the renewing of our minds are important because then we can "test and approve what God's will is." For those of us who constantly worry about knowing the will of God, Paul's answer to the problem is clear. We know God's will by learning to think as He thinks and then testing what we have learned in our daily experiences.

Renewing our minds to think as God thinks, knowing the Word of God so well that it becomes the gauge for our normal thought patterns, makes us then responsible for doing what we know.

Would you rather stew about your neighbor's behavior or look for a way to bless him? Would you rather discuss and fret about the pros and cons of a worry situation with your friends or go to God first?

Look for a way to please him. Go to God first.

What are some of the attitudes and actions you know God wants you to exhibit but you brush them aside, choosing to stay with your old flesh-nature patterns?

Love + trust is what God wants - So I am trying to do things I can't and God is disappointed and I am sinning by doing what is his work as I pray if I have faith

How does this "old" way of thinking and acting contribute to the worry in your life?

It steals our peace causes us to loose sleep, make mistakes, sets us up for physical problems and compounds stress.

To break the power of sinful thought patterns, we have to replace them with God-patterned thinking. What are some of the ways you know you will have to think differently to break the worry thought patterns in your mind?

Trust by focusing on God and knowing he will fix it or give us guidance pray instead of worry - Give it to him.

How do you feel about the cost of making such a change in your life? For instance, would your friends still be your friends if you stopped worrying along with them?

Yes. My friends want me to trust God and stop taking my time trying to fix what I control or change.

What do you see as the benefits of the change?

Peace – rest – time for God to be able to guide me to important, rewarding thoughts. It would free me from my sin.

A Closer Look at My Own Heart

Do we really want to give up the worry in our lives, or are we just "flirting" with a nice change that would be welcome if we could do it without too much effort? This question probes our hearts and minds.

An acquaintance told about her handsome, intelligent older brother who led a very full life. Suddenly his life changed when he was informed, "Larry, you have cancer." From that moment on, everything Larry thought or did, all his energy, focused on getting rid of the cancer that was slowly destroying his body.

As she finished telling about her brother's drive to become cancer free, my acquaintance added, "I wonder why we're not just as aggressive about getting rid of the sin in our lives. I guess we don't really believe the damage it does in us, how it eats away at our lives."

How does your heart respond to the thought, *Worry is a type of spiritual cancer that needs to be dealt with in my life?* Do you care enough to do what must be done?

I keep working on it. But I need to be more faithful + see it as sin like it is. That and regain my self control that seems to be lost.

In John 6:29, the people asked Jesus what they needed to do in order to do the works of God. Jesus replied, "The work of God is this: to believe in the one he has sent." The choice to be free from worry, the decision to learn what must be learned, the willingness to renew our minds—all this work is only possible through our belief in Jesus Christ and the reality of His life within us.

For your own encouragement, write out Paul's words from Philippians 4:13.

I can do everything through him who gives me strength.

Now your work is to believe in the One whose Spirit lives within you to give you strength to be free from worry. As you believe in Him enough to obey His Words concerning worry, you will sense His strength being released in and through you.

Action Steps I Can Take Today

It requires work to believe. The main battle in our war to be free from worry will be to believe enough to do what needs to be done. Jesus *has* already defeated worry; we *are* set free. For us to fully experience that freedom, our minds will need to be reprogrammed to agree with His mind. The struggle comes as our minds become an arena where the inevitable clash between believing or disbelieving Jesus Christ occurs.

Review 1 Corinthians 10:13. Who is the way of escape God has provided for us in our battle against worry's temptations?

God himself is faithful.

In order to learn from Jesus, we have to believe that His Words are true and will work. Why do you think Paul wrote "God is faithful" in the middle of this verse? What does that mean to you?

It means he is always there for us no matter how sinful all we have to do is follow and trust, obey.

When circumstances push at us, crying for resolution, demanding that we fret and fix, what promise in 1 Corinthians 10:13 lets us know that we will be able to bear the pressure without sinning?

He promises he will not let us be tempted more than we can bear. If we are He will provide a way to stand up under it.

It is difficult but necessary that you think, *I will look away from this and turn my face toward God. I will trust Him and not be afraid.* Do you have a person or situation pushing you right now? Write down what's pressuring you, and then ask God to help you believe enough in His way of escape to act on it.

Aging & illness for both Dick and I. I need to give it to God who has ALWAYS shown me a way to be strong and do what needs to me done. I must hand it over so we can enjoy this very special time. Lighten up. God has given me so many for support. Shame on me!

As part of renewing your mind, rethink your attitude toward worry. How has it changed since participating in this study?

From day one it is much better but I still have miles to go. I will work harder & be more thankful for each day.

When worry waves come, they try to knock us down, sweep us under and pull us away from God. Like the waves at the ocean shore, worry waves can be powerful and threatening.

When ocean waves get large, I leave the beach, because the waves intimidate me. But a few years ago in California, while retreating from the beach, I saw several people running toward the water, long boards under their arms, crying, "Surf's up!" What made me afraid made them excited. The huge waves meant they could use their surfboards and experience the exhilaration of a thrilling ride.

So it is with the worry waves. If we learn Scripture verses that turn our thoughts toward God and encourage us to trust Him, when the worry waves come, we can use those waves to ride right into His presence. All we need to do is begin reciting our memorized verses, and they become our "Scripture surfboards." We recognize a worry wave has come up; we take our Scripture surfboard, stand on it and ride the wave rather than letting it wash over us.

The surfer has to learn to know his surfboard; surfer and board need to move as one in order to stay on top of the waves. The following are some Scripture surfboards for you to learn. The italicized words following each verse are suggested ways to personalize the passages.

You will keep him in perfect peace, whose mind is stayed on You, because he trusts in You (Isaiah 26:3, *NKJV*). *Thank You, Lord, for keeping me in perfect peace as my mind is set on You because I will to trust You.*

Seek first the kingdom of God and His righteousness, and all these things shall be added to you (Matthew 6:33, *NKJV*). *Thank You, Lord, that as I seek You first and praise You, I will know what to do about the things nagging at me.*

The work of God is this: to believe in the one he has sent (John 6:29). *It is work for me to believe in You, Lord, when problems press for my attention, but I choose to put my trust in You.*

For God has not given us a spirit of fear, but of power and of love and of a sound mind (2 Timothy 1:7, *NKJV*). *Thank You, Lord, that You don't give me a spirit of fear, but of power and love and a sound mind.*

Continue to pray for the one you are asking God to set free from worry.

Ann explained to Ken how frightened she was of what might happen if her job were terminated. Ken advised, "Just imagine the worst that could happen and figure out what you would do then. That will take care of your fear."

Does imagining the worst and then imagining possible solutions really deal with the worry and fear in our lives? In the next chapter, we'll look at where we spend our mind time and how that affects our ability to be free from worry.

SIX

SPINNING DAYDREAMS, FEEDING NIGHTMARES

"I spend all my time thinking about what will happen if Ed doesn't get disability payments for his heart condition. How will we manage with the monthly bills and two small children to raise? Keeping busy helps, but as soon as I get quiet, fear and worry take over my thoughts."

What do we think about when we don't have anything to think about? Our answer supplies a key to the nature of our thoughts. Ask yourself these questions: *Where does my mind spend its free time? Do I spin daydreams of what might be or what might have been? Do I dwell on terrible things that could happen, filling my mind with real or imagined horrors from books, television shows or the newspaper?*

God has done all He can do to help us reject worry. When we accepted His gift of salvation through Jesus Christ, we received the Spirit of Christ to live in us. This Holy Spirit enabled Jesus to defeat all sin, including the sin of worry, and now lives in us, so we can enforce the reality of that victory in our own lives. We have been given the mind of Christ—the ability to think as He does—to guide our thought processes, and we have God's Word to fill our minds with Godlike thinking. Now we face the choice of what we will do with the provisions we have been given. Will our thinking say yes to Satan's lies, or will we choose to agree with and live out the truths of God?

Before we look more closely at our part in becoming free from worry, let's pray: "Lord, I want to have a quiet mind where my thoughts are in harmony with Yours. Please show me how to receive Your truth and how to reject the enemy's lies. Amen."

A Closer Look at the Problem

We often hear the expression, "You are what you eat," but the Bible tells us that we are what we think. What we feed our mind becomes the foundation of our thought lives. Our thought lives determine who and what we will become. To have a renewed mind, a mind not churning with anxious thoughts, we need a healthy thought diet. Such a diet will in turn lead to an unhurried, unworried lifestyle.

Remember reading Romans 8:6? "The mind of sinful man is death, but the mind controlled by the Spirit is life and peace." We've learned that the ability to have a Spirit-controlled mind becomes ours when we make Jesus Christ our Lord and Savior. So we have the ability, but how do we use that ability?

Even when a Christian recognizes worry as sin and understands how Christ's Spirit lives in him or her to overcome that sin, there is a lack of understanding as to how the battle is to be fought. Too often we think we must grit our teeth and try not to worry. The world battles that way, relying on human determination to overcome a problem or bad habit. However, the children of the kingdom of God rely on Christ's Spirit within them to help them win battles:

> For though we live in the world, we do not wage war as the world does. The weapons we fight with are not the weapons of the world. On the contrary, they have divine power to demolish strongholds. We demolish arguments and every pretension that sets itself up against the knowledge of God, and we take captive every thought to make it obedient to Christ (2 Corinthians 10:3-5).

Although we live in this world—in a carnal, fleshly body—what does Paul make clear about the way we are to fight spiritual wars?

_____

_____

_____

_____

Why should we regard the battle against worry as a spiritual battle?

_____

_____

_____

_____

The world's ways always fall short of a full and lasting victory when they are used to attempt war against sin sickness. Often the world's way of dealing with spiritual problems only masks the source of our struggle.

This is not to say we are never to go to a doctor or take medication to help us through an anxious time. God does use doctors and medicine, but they are at best a temporary means for relief from symptoms that have a spiritual cause. The sin of worry is a "dis-ease" of the spirit that manifests itself in physical and emotional ways.

A neighbor who would fret herself into immobility was given a quieting medication to help calm her nerves. The medicine worked, and she appeared to feel better. Then I realized that in truth she had only added one more worry to her list: running out of her medicine and not being able to get any more. The spiritual root of her anxiety was not removed although the medication quieted her physical symptoms.

Spiritual sins, to be dealt with effectively, must be dealt with by spiritual means. Some physical helps such as medication and exercise may contribute to a temporary relief as we learn to face and break worry's hold on our lives, but remember that a symptom relieved does not mean anxiety's defeat.

What are some of the ways you use to relieve the worry symptoms in your life? Is the relief long-lasting or temporary? How do you feel about symptom control versus the cost of getting to the root cause of the worry in your life?

_____

_____

_____

_____

How does Paul describe the power of the weapons that we use in spiritual battles?

_____

_____

_____

_____

If fear and worry have strongholds on our thoughts and actions, they have established spiritual strongholds that can only be broken down by our

acting through the power of Christ within us. What does Paul say we are
to demolish? To take captive?

_____

_____

_____

_____

_____

Why are these directions so important?

_____

_____

_____

_____

_____

Although we live in a fleshly body, we can't fight temptation with our
fleshly abilities. Instead, we are to stand against temptation by choosing
to cooperate with the divinely powerful Spirit within us, knowing that He
has won the victory over all temptation.

Anytime we allow our minds to dwell on things contrary to the truths
of God, we open our thinking to the lies of the enemy. All too often we
spend our free-mind time in pretentious daydreaming. We take our Mary
Poppins's bag of pretend and spin wondrous imaginations. Or like the
foolish man who took the bale of hay to bed to feed his nightmares, we
collect our bale of troubles and take them to bed to feed our mind during
our wakeful night hours.

In Psalm 119:113 the psalmist writes, "I hate vain thoughts: but thy
law do I love" (KJV). One of the greatest challenges we face when we want
to be free from worry is learning to hate our vain thoughts—to hate them
so much that we will do whatever we need to do to be rid of them.

Identify some of the vain thoughts you have been entertaining this past
week. Why do you spend your mind time on these thoughts?

_____

_____

_____

_____

_____

A Closer Look at God's Truth

The renewing of our minds by refusing thoughts contrary to Christ's mind within us is an ongoing process. In order to agree with the mind of Christ and resist the temptation to worry, we *learn* to take our daily (and nightly) thoughts captive, keeping those thoughts that are of God and refusing others that trigger worry. This process of controlling our thought lives involves persistent and painful practice, but the Holy Spirit stands ready to empower us to keep on until we experience the victory He has won. Remember, we are divinely empowered for the destruction of fear and worry strongholds.

Read James 1:2-4. What do you think of James's challenge to us concerning how we face our trials?

_____

_____

_____

_____

Remember the difference between my reaction to the ocean waves in California and the reaction of the surfers in chapter 5? Think about how your anxiety compares to a surfer's delight. How is it possible for you to consider a trial that causes worry as a source of joy?

_____

_____

_____

_____

In the United States, we live in a society of instant everything. To endure through a testing in order for patience to develop and do its good work contradicts the mindset that expects immediate results. How do you respond to the need for patient practice in order to bring your worry under control?

_____

_____

_____

_____

Review 1 Corinthians 10:13. Remembering that no temptation can come our way except what God allows and that He has promised to make a way for us to bear it, how can waves of worry prove these truths?

_____

_____

_____

_____

_____

How can worry waves show the reliability of your Scripture surfboards (memorized verses)?

_____

_____

_____

_____

_____

Worry waves, or trials, test our faith, and if we will allow them to do so, they will also build our endurance. The temptations to worry can become a proving ground for our faith in God's way of escape and our trust in His faithfulness. When we agree with the mind of Christ within us, allowing His Spirit to empower us to speak faith instead of worry, we test and affirm the will of our God.

From Romans 12:2, remember how the renewing of our mind enables us to prove God's good, pleasing and perfect will. As we see God's Word work against worry, our faith grows. The stronger we become in believing we can stand against the temptation to worry, the greater will be our sense of His power within us. We'll know victory is really ours, just as He promises.

A Closer Look at My Own Heart

Read James 1:12-15. How does this passage show that temptation is normal for the Christian?

_____

_____

_____

_____

Paul wrote, "No temptation has seized you except what is common to man" (1 Corinthians 10:13). Now James tells us that anyone who endures temptation is blessed because of the results that will occur as his or her faith is proven.

Temptation is not sin, but it invites us to sin. Becoming a Christian does not set us free from temptation, but it does empower us to resist the temptation, so we do not sin. Both the temptation to worry and the sin itself are so prevalent in the Body of Christ that we tend to accept it as normal behavior. The "everybody does it" excuse causes us to rationalize away the command of Jesus, "Do not worry."

What temptations to worry are plaguing you today? Identify the temptations that you have allowed to go beyond temptation into the sin of worry. Using your personal examples, describe the difference between temptation and sin as you understand it.

_____

_____

_____

_____

Blessed is the person who continues on the journey of becoming free from worry, putting one foot ahead of the other, step by step, choice by choice. Blessed is the one who endures temptation or, as James 1:12 says, "who perseveres under trial." Why does breaking down strongholds of worry and taking captive every vain imagination require endurance? What kind of endurance does freeing ourselves from worry require of you personally?

_____

_____

_____

_____

The dictionary definition of "persevere" is "to persist . . . in spite of counterinfluences, opposition, or discouragement." What kind of counterinfluences, opposition or discouragement does Satan bring against our decisions not to worry?

_____

_____

_____

Why can we resist Satan?

_____

_____

_____

_____

_____

According to verse 14 in James 1, what causes us to be drawn into temptation?

_____

_____

_____

_____

I've had people say to me, "Just imagine the worst thing that could happen in the situation, accept it and then you won't have to worry about it anymore." One of my greatest difficulties concerning worry has been my refusal to not finish a worry scenario. As the what-if started in my head, instead of stopping it immediately, I would go on and play it out to the bitter end, thinking that concluding the thought might stop the anxiety. It seemed like a way to be in control, at least in my imagination.

I finally learned that the what-if beginning thought is like a hook, and the following thoughts of what might happen and how I'd react were the line and sinker. I saw how I'd been swallowing the enemy's propaganda—hook, line and sinker. My desire to work out a solution for the what-if (in case it did happen) had drawn me into entertaining thoughts that were destructive to my spiritual health.

Identify a recent "hook, line and sinker" scenario in which you imagined a possible problem and solution. How much mind time did you spend on it?

_____

_____

_____

_____

_____

It's possible, if we're really experienced at imagining, to do the whole process in seconds. Did you feel more in control after the imagined solution? Why or why not?

_____

_____

_____

_____

Our daughter came home with the news that she and Larry had set their wedding date. "I've a whole, wonderful year to get ready," she exclaimed.

I thought, *And I have a whole year to worry about all the details.*

I spent much of my time during the year making backup plans for the what-ifs of every situation. We never needed them because all went well. Sometimes I was even a little disappointed not to have the chance to prove the need for my backup plans!

On the day of the wedding, though, something happened that I hadn't worried about. I'd never heard of such a thing occurring, or I would have had my backup plan ready.

The bridesmaids had stayed overnight with our daughter. We had two bathrooms, and we used two cars to transport everyone to the church. When the girls lined up for the processional, we found we were missing a bridesmaid. She had been primping in the bathroom when everyone left the house. Each carload thought she was with the other. It took some fancy, unplanned-for scrambling to get everyone together, but then the wedding proceeded with no more glitches.

That evening, relaxing on the couch, I thought, *This is the best part of the whole year—having it over. I don't have to worry about all those details anymore.*

It was then that the Lord began to show me what I had lost throughout the year because of my anxiety. It was then that He showed me what the sin of worry had stolen, killed and destroyed throughout my life. And it was then that I determined by God's empowering to free myself from the worry that held me in its sinful bondage.

Think for a moment why worry is a temptation to you. Since worry is sin, it can't tempt you unless you have a sinful need or desire that worry offers to satisfy. Perhaps it's a need for self-preservation or a sense of pride. You may feel like the one who "has to do the worrying around here." Why is that? Perhaps the need to feel in control leads you to explore all the what-ifs, so you can be prepared.

What tempts you to accept worry as a necessary part of your life?

_____

_____

_____

_____

_____

Remember in John 10:10, Jesus warned, "The thief comes only to steal and kill and destroy." The worry patterns that deceive us into a false sense of control are used by Satan to entrap our minds. Learning to persevere in our resistance will bring us both increased patience and a greater awareness of the power of the Holy Spirit within us.

When a doctor puts you on a diet to help correct a physical problem, he wants you to carefully follow his or her instructions. What we eat affects our physical wellbeing. In the same way, our mental diet will affect our spiritual wellbeing.

Read Philippians 4:8. What things does Paul say we are to use for our mental meditation?

_____

_____

_____

_____

_____

List some of the places where you would expect to find this kind of healthy food for your mind.

_____

_____

_____

_____

What are some places that tempt you to indulge in mental junk food?

_____

_____

_____

_____

What do you feed your mind most of the time? Why do you choose your particular kind of mental diet?

_____

_____

_____

_____

_____

Action Steps I Can Take Today

A Bible study teacher was helping her students understand the importance of only taking into their lives those things that belong to them as children of God. She asked, "What does a person do who has exited his plane and gone to the luggage area to retrieve his suitcase?"

The students answered, "He waits until the luggage from his plane comes around the conveyor belt. Then he watches until he sees his suitcase. When it gets to him, he picks it up."

Then the teacher asked, "Why doesn't he pick up one of the other suitcases?"

One of the students replied, "Why, he wouldn't do that. It's not his bag. He doesn't want luggage that doesn't belong to him."

It's so simple as to be astounding. Worry is not our "bag," so we don't pick it up.

Observe carefully what you feed your mind during the next 24 hours. What's in your mental diet that may be feeding your nightmares and encouraging you to have vain daydreams? What do you need to change in your diet? (Remember, your thought patterns reflect what you've been feeding your mind.)

From Paul's list in Philippians 4:8, create your own specific list of things on which your mind needs to dwell.

_____

_____

_____

_____

_____

_____

Practice meeting worry temptations with the thought, *That's not my bag.* Satan can't make you take what you refuse to pick up.

Memorize and meditate on Philippians 4:8. Just as you would check your doctor's diet guidelines before ordering a meal, use Paul's mental diet list before you feed your mind. It works to say to the enemy, "According to God's Word, that's not a true [or pure or admirable] thought, and I'm not taking it." Then don't!

Remember to continue praying for the one you want to see God set free from worry's bondage.

Joe met his friend Pete on the street and asked him how things were going. Pete replied, "Under the circumstances, I guess I'm getting along okay."

Responded Joe, "What in the world are you doing *under* there?"

Fear and worry always drag us under the circumstances, causing us to feel anything but victorious. In the next chapter, we'll learn one of the simplest but most effective ways God has given for us to live above our circumstances: thanksgiving. Giving thanks was never meant to be a once-a-year occasion. God gave it to us as a way of life, a way to live above our problems and free from worry's hold.

SEVEN

THANKING GOD ALWAYS

To think on things true, noble, right, pure, lovely, admirable, praiseworthy—what an assignment!

Such thinking may be possible in our prayer closets and in rare moments of calm, but what about the other 90 percent of our time: when the kids need a ride to a birthday party, dinner plans demand a trip to the store, the front tire of the car is soft again, the boss says you have to work overtime, a coworker fails to complete a job for which you are responsible? How can we think noble thoughts then?

Even in hectic times, we need not lose energy worrying. A simple but powerful scriptural key teaches us how to bring God into every situation immediately. To be free from worry in all circumstances, we need to practice this God-given key daily, often hourly, and sometimes even moment by moment.

Before we look at this further, let's pray: "Lord, teach me the importance of giving thanks to You in all things. Thank you for empowering me to do it. Amen."

A Closer Look at the Problem

When problems, big or little, come into our lives, everything in our human reasoning demands we deal with them. We respond to the demands in different ways. Some of us may climb into bed and pull the covers over our heads, escaping the unpleasantness in sleep. Workaholics find more work to do so they won't have time to face the problem. Still others jump right into finding (and worrying about) a reasonable solution.

God's way of handling a problem differs greatly from our man-made designs for coping. God tells us to come to Him immediately, the instant we sense a problem developing.

Two sisters were learning to knit. As usual with beginners, the yarn would knot, stitches would be dropped, and a sense of frustration would develop. One sister, a very determined individual, worked and worked at repairing the place where a stitch was lost, all the while causing her yarn to become more entangled. Finally, when she realized things were only getting worse, she went to her mother for help. Sighing, the mother looked at her daughter's handiwork and said, "Why didn't you come to me as soon as you saw you had a problem? It would have been much easier to fix then. Now we have to take out several rows and spend time getting the yarn untangled."

The other sister, hearing the conversation, decided to come to her mother right then for help. "See," she said, "I think something's wrong here, but I'm not sure what. Before I make a mess, will you tell me what to do?"

The mother showed her daughter how she had twisted a stitch and quickly had her back at her knitting. An hour later, the mother had also managed to correct the other sister's mistakes, untangle her yarn and set her to knitting again.

As the mother left the room, she reminded both girls, "Remember, come to me the minute you think you have a problem. Don't try to figure it out by yourselves. If you come to me at once, you'll save us all a lot of unnecessary frustration."

When Jesus calls us out of something like worry, He always calls us into something to replace what we left behind. Read Matthew 11:28-30. Who did Jesus invite to come to Him?

_____

_____

_____

_____

_____

We know how weary and burdened we get by the worry in our lives. What would happen if we went to Jesus before we got so burdened by our problems?

_____

_____

_____

_____

_____

How would you feel if you had peace at the beginning of a problem and throughout its hard places as well as at its end? How do you think staying close to Jesus would accomplish this?

_____

_____

_____

_____

What did Jesus say we must do in order to experience His promised rest?

_____

_____

_____

Think of the mother whose two daughters were learning to knit. What is the yoke in their relationship? How would this enable the girls to learn from their mother?

_____

_____

_____

_____

When oxen are yoked together as a team, they are made to work in harmony by a physical yoke, literally fastening them to one another. The mother in our story wanted her daughters to stay closely yoked with her in their learning process, so they could follow her directions. How does such a yoking—whether to a teacher, a mentor or Jesus—contribute to the learning process?

_____

_____

_____

If we understand that our soul is made up of mind, will and emotions, what did Jesus mean when He promised rest for our soul?

_____

_____

_____

Where do worry temptations plague us most, and where do they find a foothold? Why are we so vulnerable in our souls?

_____

_____

_____

_____

Our minds, wills and emotions comprise the decision-making part of who we are. The Spirit of God in us will always want us to think and act God's way. Our fleshly bodies will always want us to satisfy our human desires. So even as God wants to renew our minds to think as He does, Satan's temptations entice our minds to continue the sinful thoughts that lead to sinful actions. Sin's temptations seem to thrive in our emotions. God's principles thrive in our renewed minds. The will, buffeted by both our thoughts and our emotions, will choose to set itself either toward God or away from Him. In our desire to be free from worry, we are learning to resist worry's temptation as it tries to establish a foothold in our souls. By learning from Jesus, our renewed mind can overcome the sinful surges of our emotions and turn our will to obey God.

According to Matthew 11:30, how did Jesus describe His yoke and His burden?

_____

_____

_____

_____

We are never promised a problem-free life. But when we come to God first, staying close to Him as He leads us through the difficulties, there will be a peace in the process that only God can give. We will not become worry weary and fall into discouragement and depression. Of course, we will become physically tired at times, but only spiritual "dis-ease" burdens us with anxiety and despair.

A Closer Look at God's Truth

When our souls—mind, will and emotions—are in turmoil, our way of trying to bring peace is to solve the problem plaguing us. Much of our weariness in life comes from having our minds on situations rather than on God. When the responsibility seems more than we can bear, then we become "me-centered" and worry multiplies. To save us from this self-centered pattern, Jesus says, "Come to Me."

Too often we respond, "Right after I get this problem settled, Lord; then I'll come and we'll be able to have fellowship again." Probably Martha planned to have time to sit with Jesus after the demands of the meal were over. Jesus wanted her to discover the joy of being yoked in fellowship with Him *first*. Then the preparation of the meal would fall into its proper place, and the heaviness of her over-responsible attitude would be lightened. The effectiveness of Martha's serving gift would be enhanced because she took time first to learn from Jesus.

Today we say to an overly anxious person, "Why don't you lighten up?" Name some areas in your life where you see a need to lighten up by listening to Jesus more than listening to the demands of a situation.

_____

_____

_____

_____

What worry problem are you focusing on solving, thinking that when you finally get it taken care of you'll be able to concentrate on your relationship with the Lord again? How do you feel about His urging you to concentrate on Him *now*?

_____

_____

_____

_____

Read 1 Thessalonians 5:16-18. When we begin to move from the heavy yoke of worry about our problems to the lighter yoke of obedience to God, the practice of certain biblical principles will help us keep our focus. What command is given the believer in verse 16?

_____

_____

_____

_____

Why would we prefer this be a suggestion rather than a command?

_____

_____

_____

_____

How do you feel about this seemingly unreal expectation of Paul?

_____

_____

_____

_____

_____

Compare this command with Paul's words in Philippians 4:4. What (or who) are we to be joyful about?

_____

_____

_____

_____

Name some of the things about God that are worthy of our rejoicing, regardless of how difficult our immediate circumstances may be.

_____

_____

_____

_____

Why do we find it hard to obey this command when we're worried and troubled about many things?

_____

_____

_____

_____

If Paul's words offered a suggestion, we would only need to be joyful when we feel great, things are right in our world, and God is doing things we want. But think about the power rejoicing has over worry. Can rejoicing and worry coexist? Why do you think God wants us to rejoice *always* in who He is and what He has done for us?

How could rejoicing be used as a spiritual weapon against worry?

According to 1 Thessalonians 5:17, how much is the believer to pray?

Prayer is an attitude of the heart, not just our talking to God. A heart always open to God—ready to hear Him or speak to Him—is a heart praying continually. Prayer is an attitude of continual openness to God, not just the continual speaking of words. Review our "Scripture surfboard" from Isaiah 26:3. How does that verse fit with our description of a person praying continually?

Notice that in 1 Thessalonians 5:18, Paul commanded us to be thankful *in* all circumstances, not *for* all circumstances. Francis Frangipane writes in *The Three Battlegrounds*, "The Lord is never worried, never in a hurry nor without an answer."[1] When we recognize this about God, what kind of thanks can we give, in spite of our circumstances? Why?

Remember the story of Joe and his friend Pete at the end of chapter 6? How do you think giving thanks in the midst of our problems enables us to rise above the circumstances?

_____

_____

_____

_____

Psalm 50:23 says, "He who sacrifices thank offerings honors me, and he prepares the way so that I may show him the salvation of God." The giving of thanks turns our focus from ourselves and our problems to God and His in-control faithfulness. When we give thanks in the midst of our struggles, we are giving thanks sacrificially. God's Word says that when we give the sacrifice of thanksgiving, we make the way ready for God to show us His way of salvation in our difficulties.

What do you think happens in us when we make the sacrificial effort to show thankfulness to God?

_____

_____

_____

_____

How does this prepare us to receive God's way of salvation?

_____

_____

_____

_____

I'm not an easily depressed person, but when I allow worry and its accompanying depression a foothold in my life, I feel as if I will be under its dark cloud forever. Having learned the way of escape, I can choose to take it. When I do, deliverance always comes.

My way of escape goes like this: "Thank You, Lord, for this day You have given. Thank You that I can get out of bed, even when I don't want to do so. Thank You for hot running water, for a toothbrush and toothpaste, for cereal and milk to put on it, for clothes to wear, for a house to clean and for food to feed my family."

Nothing is too small for me to ignore in my thanksgiving way of escape. In fact, the smaller the details, the more I begin to enjoy discovering the blessings in seemingly unimportant things. Sometimes, if I've really let worry and depression get a foothold, I may have to practice thanksgiving for two or three days. But always the darkness lifts, and my thanksgiving turns from a sacrificial act of obedience to a heartfelt response to God's goodness.

Notice that I was the one who let the worry hang around long enough to induce depression. I'd neglected or deliberately ignored the commands to rejoice, to keep my heart open to God and to give thanks because I was fretting about some worrisome situation. But God, in His grace, still offered me a way of escape; and as I began to move in the smallest acts of thankful obedience, He showed me His salvation.

Remember the closing words of 1 Thessalonians 5:16-18? We are to be joyful always, pray continually, and give thanks in all circumstances, for this is God's will for us in Christ Jesus. Why do you think we are reminded that this type of thankful obedience is only possible "in Christ Jesus"?

_____

_____

_____

_____

_____

When these commands seem impossible to us, from whom will we get strength (see Philippians 4:13)?

_____

_____

_____

_____

_____

Why is it so important to remember this Scripture surfboard when a tidal wave of worry strikes?

_____

_____

_____

_____

Why do you think it's important to practice on the little worry waves that come our way?

_____

_____

_____

_____

_____

Let's look at 2 Chronicles 20:1-30 to see how the principles we've been studying worked out in the experience of King Jehoshaphat.

When the Moabites and Ammonites came to make war against Judah, the Scriptures tell us that King Jehoshaphat was alarmed—and he *resolved* to inquire of the Lord. As the king and the people gathered, the king prayed, "O LORD, God of our Fathers, are you not the God who is in heaven? You rule over all the kingdoms of the nations. Power and might are in your hand, and no one can withstand you" (verse 6).

How does the beginning of King Jehoshaphat's prayer illustrate the way we are to begin overcoming fear and worry in a situation?

_____

_____

_____

_____

In the middle of his prayer, what promise of God did the king use as a reason for his expecting God to hear and act on Judah's behalf?

_____

_____

_____

_____

How does that promise compare with the one we are given in 1 Corinthians 10:13?

_____

_____

_____

_____

Following Jehoshaphat's prayer, we are told that the Spirit of the Lord came upon one of the men in the gathering and that the man said the following:

> Do not be afraid or discouraged because of this vast army. For the battle is not yours, but God's. . . . You will not have to fight this battle. Take up your positions; stand firm and see the deliverance the LORD will give you. . . . Do not be afraid; do not be discouraged. Go out to face them tomorrow, and the LORD will be with you (2 Chronicles 20:15-17).

Even though the Lord had said the battle was His and the Israelites wouldn't have to fight, what did God expect them to do?

_____

_____

_____

_____

Why do you think God commanded the Israelites to take up their positions?

_____

_____

_____

_____

Why was it important that the Israelites stand firm?

_____

_____

_____

_____

In verses 18 and 19, how did the king and the people respond? What did their actions say about how they had received the words spoken through God's messenger?

_____

_____

_____

_____

_____

The next morning the army prepared to set out for the battleground. What did the king say would determine their victory (see verse 20)?

_____

_____

_____

According to verse 21, who went out at the head of the army? What did they do?

_____

_____

_____

According to verse 22, when did the Lord move to turn the men in the enemy's army against each other? How does this situation illustrate the scriptural truth that God honors those who honor Him?

_____

_____

_____

According to verses 27 and 28, where did the king and the people of Judah go after God gave them victory over their enemies?

_____

_____

_____

How was thanksgiving woven throughout this whole episode? What effect did the king's resolve have on God? On the people? On the outcome of the problem?

_____

_____

_____

_____

According to verses 29 and 30, what effects reached beyond the solution to the original problem?

_____

_____

_____

What does this tell us about the outcome of our problems if we resolve to begin with thanksgiving, to walk through the difficulties with thanksgiving and then, when the problems are solved, to let thanksgiving overflow in praise to God?

_____

_____

_____

A Closer Look at My Own Heart

It's easy to agree in our minds that rejoicing, praying and giving thanks are weapons against the worry thoughts that try to invade our thinking. It's easy to sit with a group and talk about practicing all these good principles we're learning. But how will we do when God brings us into a practice arena where we can learn in our experience the reality of the truth we've accepted with our heads?

An Olympic gold-medal skater, Scott Hamilton, did a TV special on the training involved in becoming a champion skater. One of the most memorable shots showed Scott standing on the ice in the middle of a large, empty arena. Stretching out his arms, Scott said something like this: "If it doesn't happen here, it won't happen out there." Then he went on to explain the hours of practice needed when no crowd, no judges, no praise filled the arena—only the skater, the ice and the empty bleachers. If the practice didn't take place there, neither would the sweetness of victory occur during competition.

Why is practicing the principles related to being set free from worry so important?

_____

_____

Are you willing to practice being free from worry in the arena where you are now? What about your particular situation might cause you to hesitate?

_____

_____

_____

Read Psalm 34:1-4. How do David's words line up with the commands Paul gave us as believers today?

_____

_____

_____

_____

At the time of this psalm, David was running from King Saul. Saul continually tried to kill David, and God continually delivered David. These verses show how David overcame the temptation to worry during this time in his life. How does David's use of the word "will" signify his determination?

_____

_____

_____

_____

How often did David determine to give praise and thanksgiving to God?

_____

_____

_____

_____

From what we have learned, why was it important that giving God praise and thanksgiving be a regular practice for David?

_____

_____

_____

_____

Read Psalm 103:1-5. How did David use self-talk to encourage himself in practicing praise and thanksgiving?

_____

_____

_____

_____

Sometimes, when no other person is around to encourage us, we have to encourage ourselves in the Lord. We need to say, "Soul, you will praise the

Lord." Giving thanks is not a matter of *feeling* thankful but of *choosing to be* thankful.

Write an example of how you might talk to yourself to bring your soul into obediently (not necessarily "feelingly") offering a sacrifice of thanksgiving to God.

_____

_____

_____

_____

In Acts 16:22-40, we read about a time when Paul and Silas were beaten and thrown into prison because the Jews stirred up a mob against their teaching. The jailer "put them in the inner cell and fastened their feet in the stocks" (verse 24). Now think about their response to this situation: "About midnight Paul and Silas were praying and singing hymns to God, and the other prisoners were listening to them" (verse 25).

The Bible relates how suddenly an earthquake shook the prison, all the prisoners were freed, and the doors opened. But no one left. The jailer, ready to kill himself because he thought all his prisoners had fled, became a follower of Jesus as a result of the salvation he saw God bring to Paul and Silas.

What prepared the way of God's salvation, not only for Paul and Silas, but for the jailer and his family as well?

_____

_____

_____

_____

Although Paul and Silas had been harshly treated and their situation looked very dim indeed, they *chose* to pray and sing hymns to God. What does this say to us about the problems that seem to imprison us, our no-light-at-the-end-of-the-tunnel situations? How does this story encourage sacrificial thanksgiving?

_____

_____

_____

How about your situation? Why do you feel it is too hard for you to give
the sacrifice of thanksgiving?

_____

_____

_____

_____

Do you feel justified in holding on to your fear, your anger, your worry?
Why?

_____

_____

_____

_____

Look again at David's words in Psalms 34 and 103 and at the behavior of
Paul and Silas in Acts 16. Reread Philippians 4:13. How was Paul enabled
to give thanks? How can you? Will you choose to do it?

_____

_____

_____

_____

_____

Action Steps I Can Take Today

David, Paul and Silas didn't learn to rejoice, pray and offer thanksgiving
overnight. Paul told those he taught, "Whatever you have learned or received or heard from me, or seen in me—put it into practice. And the God
of peace will be with you" (Philippians 4:9). Notice Paul affirmed that the
God of peace will be with you *even while you're practicing*, not just when you
get it right or have become accomplished at defeating worry's temptations.
So let's do some practicing.

As you go about your day's responsibilities and feel the pressure of
hurry and worry building up, deliberately take a few minutes to sit down
and turn your thoughts toward thanking God.

Your human thinking will try to convince you to wait until you are
caught up and have time, but don't let that kind of thinking trap you.
Remind yourself that God is never hurried or worried and that He has

everything under control. Then drawing on your Scripture surfboard Philippians 4:13 ("I can do everything through him who gives me strength"), deliberately choose to stop hurrying and sit for a few moments. Use rejoicing, prayer and thanksgiving to turn your mind from what you think needs to be done to the One who is worthy of your praise.

Rest in His presence for a few minutes, until you are quieted inside as well as out. Then get up and continue your work. If the hurry-worry pressure builds again, repeat the rejoice-pray-thanksgiving process. Remember, you *are* practicing, you *are* learning, and you *will* be free from worry.

When you find yourself stuck someplace—at a stoplight, in a telephone conversation, in the check-out line at the grocery store, in a dull meeting—instead of looking at your watch and fretting, begin to give thanks:

Thank You, Lord, that You know right where I am now. Thank You that my times are in Your hands and I can trust You with the unfolding of my day. Thank You for this chance to practice being yoked together with You, drawing on Your rest. Amen.

Make up your own thanksgiving phrases or add to those suggested, but turn your focus from the frustration of waiting to the wonder of God's caring for you right where you are. Repeat this process as often as necessary throughout the day.

Learn this new Scripture surfboard from 1 Thessalonians 5:16-18: "Be joyful always; pray continually; give thanks in all circumstances, for this is God's will for you in Christ Jesus." Learn to pray the Scripture in your own words:

Lord, I choose to be joyful because I belong to You, to keep my heart open to pray continually and to give thanks in all my circumstances for this is Your will for me as I am strengthened by Christ Jesus.

⁓ ✦ ⁓

A few weeks after a *Free from Worry* Bible study ended, Dianne called the teacher. "I'm having a really hard time," she said. "While we were meeting every week, I did fine practicing what we were learning. But now I can't seem to keep doing it, and my old worry habits are coming back. I believed I was free from worry's hold on me, but I need to know how to stay free."

Most of us have experienced the joy of losing weight on a diet and then the disappointment when the weight came back as our discipline began to slip. In the next chapter, we'll look at some of the challenges to be faced as we practice being free from worry, and we'll look at some tips for helping us maintain our freedom from worry no matter where we find ourselves.

Note

1. Francis Frangipane, *The Three Battlegrounds* (Cedar Rapids, IA: Arrow Publications, 2006).

STAYING FREE

Freedom from worry is a gift from God, purchased by Jesus Christ through His death on the cross. Like all gifts, this freedom needs to be appreciated and exercised if it is to bring the fullness of life Jesus speaks about in John 10:10: "I have come that they may have life, and have it to the full."

Our "faith muscles" are very similar to our physical ones. Exercise and proper care will cause our faith muscles to grow and toughen until we can take on increasingly more difficult challenges. But neglect and careless indifference can cause us to lose even the little strength we have begun to develop against worry's temptations.

The apostle Paul wrote these words to Timothy: "Train yourself to be godly. For physical training is of some value, but godliness has value for all things, holding promise for both the present life and the life to come" (1 Timothy 4:7-8).

Our human thinking and human flesh do not like being subject to the discipline of God's Word. Our human nature will use every opportunity to reassert itself and take back the control it lost when we chose to obey God, and Satan himself will challenge us. Therefore, it's important that our spiritual training continue even when we are away from our Bible study group or separated from encouraging friends, for the same scriptural truths about worry apply whether we are by ourselves or we participate in a study group. We are to train ourselves to be godly, even in the most private times of our lives where no one sees or hears us but God.

Before we go on, let's take the time to pray: "Lord, thank You for showing me how to be free from worry. Please make me aware of any tendency to return to its bondage, and show me how to escape the desire to give up when I get tired of Your training. Amen."

A Closer Look at the Problem

Jesus said to the Jews who had believed Him, "If you hold to my teaching, you are really my disciples. Then you will know the truth, and the truth will set you free" (John 8:31-32).

What does it means to hold to the teachings of Jesus?

_____

_____

_____

_____

How does holding to Jesus' teachings exhibit a faith beyond casual acceptance?

_____

_____

_____

_____

There is a recognizable pattern in the way God builds our faith muscles. As we begin to learn a new truth and gather the courage to step out and test it in our experience, we are rewarded with some instant results. Our faith flares up, much like a newly struck match, and we declare with enthusiasm our desire to live by this truth every day of our lives.

But after granting a few flares of faith, God begins to lengthen the time between the faith-building results. He is looking for a steady faith flame that won't go out. Will we "hold to" the truth we so eagerly embraced in the beginning, or will we become discouraged when the frequency of immediate results lessens? This is the time when our determination to "know the truth" is tested.

For those of us becoming free from worry, being tested means exercising the principles of escape we have learned, even when we don't see immediate results. We have entered the practice arena where there are no crowds, no instant victories—nothing and no one but us and God's Word working in us. We fall and get up, and we fall again and get up again. The important part of the practice is the getting up and doing it again. The truth about worry that we have accepted with our mind is being tested and tried as the Holy Spirit works that truth into the very fabric of our beings.

What steps have we learned to take when we find we have fallen into worry?

_____

_____

_____

_____

Why are repentance and receiving forgiveness necessary in our getting up again and continuing in our quest to be free from the bondage of worry?

_____

_____

_____

The psalmist wrote of Joseph during his slavery and imprisonment in Egypt: "Till what [God] foretold came to pass, till the word of the LORD proved [Joseph] true" (Psalm 105:19). After many trials and many years in which Joseph held to God's Word, he became second in command over all of Egypt, and his brothers bowed down to him as God had said they would. As we keep on practicing, letting the words of God concerning worry prove us, we will eventually see freedom from worry become a way of life—a full life, just as Jesus promised.

Many Christians refer to a season when a truth of God is being tested and proven in their lives as a dry time. By being aware of the pattern of faith growth, a dry time won't cause you to give up in despair. Instead, you will recognize what's happening and know you are moving slowly but surely into freedom from worry's bondage.

How do you think your understanding of the truth about worry will change as you continue practicing during a dry time, even when circumstances seem to deny the validity of that truth?

_____

_____

_____

_____

Why would the truth have power to set you free in a way that was not there when you started your faith walk?

_____

_____

_____

_____

An overweight young woman finally acknowledged her problem and sought a doctor's help. After a difficult year of adjusting to the doctor's diet and exercise program, she reached the normal weight for her height and age. As the doctor released her, he cautioned, "You need to maintain a balanced diet and moderate exercise program, and see me yearly for a checkup. It's essential you continue the good habits you've established if you want to keep your weight down."

How does this story illustrate our need to continue practicing the godly principles we have learned in this study?

_____

_____

_____

The apostle Paul wrote, "But as for you, continue in what you have learned and have become convinced of" (2 Timothy 3:14). What are some of the things you may have a hard time giving up as you become free from worry?

_____

_____

_____

_____

Why do you think the writers of the New Testament felt it necessary to constantly encourage believers to keep on in the faith?

_____

_____

_____

_____

A Closer Look at God's Truth

As our world becomes more confusing and dangerous, we hear the argument that anyone would worry in today's world. Such reasoning implies that if we don't know enough to worry, we are foolish.

Hebrews 13:8 says, "Jesus Christ is the same yesterday and today and forever." What does this verse make clear about our troubling todays?

_____

_____

_____

_____

How does this verse affirm the ability of Christ's Spirit in us being able to keep us from worry no matter how troubled our times?

_____

_____

_____

_____

Remember that if it is truly more difficult to live without worrying in to-day's society, God will give us more grace and all the strength we need to obey Him.

In John 8:36, Jesus said, "So if the Son sets you free, you will be free indeed." Jesus had been explaining how anyone who sins is a slave to sin. His Jewish listeners were insisting that they were free because they had never been slaves to anyone.

Although we may not be slaves to *anyone*, if we worry, we are a slave to the sin of worry. But Jesus came to set us free and intends that we shall be "free indeed."

What do the words "free indeed" tell us about the kind of freedom from worry Jesus intends for us to experience?

_____

_____

_____

_____

What is the difference between having an occasional worry-free time and a lifestyle that refuses to entertain worry thoughts?

_____

_____

_____

_____

Which do you think Jesus has planned for us?

_____

_____

_____

_____

Read Hebrews 12:1-3. How do fear and anxiety fit into the admonition to "throw off everything that hinders and the sin that so easily entangles"?

_____

_____

_____

What are some of the ways worry hinders your Christian walk and entangles your thinking?

_____

_____

_____

Dolores asked an experienced speaker how she handled nervousness. In sharing with the speaker, Dolores talked about the butterflies she got every time she spoke in front of a group. Then she asked, "Do they ever go away? I get so anxious about what I'm going to say that I've almost decided to quit doing that kind of thing."

The speaker smiled and replied, "No, usually the butterflies don't go away. You just teach them to fly in formation."

How does the experienced speaker's response illustrate the discipline described in Hebrews 12:1? Although she still has the temptation to let worry symptoms control her, how has she learned to respond?

_____

_____

_____

Review Matthew 6:33. How does this verse tell us we are to keep our worry butterflies "in formation"?

_____

_____

_____

What does Hebrews 12:2 tell us to focus our attention on?

_____

_____

_____

What does Hebrews 12:3 promise us when our focus is on the right place?

_____

_____

_____

_____

What do these verses from Hebrews 12 tell us about the probability of our becoming weary and losing heart at times as we strive to be free from worry?

_____

_____

_____

How does that warning prepare us for those times?

_____

_____

_____

A Closer Look at My Own Heart

Jesus spoke often to His disciples about His coming death and resurrection. Although the disciples didn't understand all He was saying, Jesus knew it was important to tell them. He explained, "I am telling you now before it happens, so that when it does happen you will believe that I am He" (John 13:19).

Does it make you somewhat fearful and anxious to hear how your freedom from worry will be challenged? Why or why not?

_____

_____

_____

_____

My dentist had to do a root canal on one of my teeth. Having never had the surgery before and having heard some terrible tales, I told him how anxious I was. He took the time to explain to me the details of what would be happening and how I could know where we were in the process as it unfolded. He also promised to explain what he was doing as the surgery progressed.

My dentist's caring about my fear reassured me, and although I didn't really understand much of what he said, I felt comforted by his willingness to explain.

During the actual surgery, as the procedure unfolded exactly as it had been explained to me, my confidence in my dentist increased considerably. He had been honest with me. My experience proved the reliability of his words.

This final chapter of *Free from Worry* is an attempt to be honest about some of the "procedures" that will accompany our walk. Understanding some of the ways our practice will be challenged is part of the preparation for meeting those challenges. We are warned of the struggles so that when they come, our faith will be encouraged rather than discouraged.

Carefully read Ephesians 6:10-18. According to verses 10 and 11, where does our strength to stand against the enemy come from? How does this fact relate to our Philippians 4:13 surfboard?

_____

_____

_____

We often say, "You worry me" or "That situation makes me anxious." But no person or situation can *force* us to worry. Our battle isn't against certain people or problems but against the spirits of fear and worry that seek to manipulate us into sinning against God.

How does Ephesians 6:12 describe our battle? Since our flesh is helpless to fight spiritual forces, why is it important for us to recognize the power of the Spirit of Christ in us?

_____

_____

_____

_____

The word "stand" is mentioned four times in these verses. What similar attitude is reflected in holding to the truth and standing firm?

_____

_____

_____

What does Paul's use of these words indicate about the challenge we will face in our efforts to be free from worry?

_____

_____

_____

_____

Reread Ephesians 6:14-17. List the weapons that are identified as protection for us to use in the spiritual battles we will face. Beside each weapon, write how Jesus is each of the weapons.

_____

_____

_____

_____

Why is it important that we recognize we *have* these weapons in Christ Jesus?

_____

_____

_____

_____

What do you believe about these provisions? How sure are you that these weapons are personally yours?

_____

_____

_____

_____

If you feel you lack the assurance needed to use the weapons you have listed, don't be discouraged. Ask God to teach you, and He will. David wrote, "Praise be to the LORD my Rock, who trains my hands for war" (Psalm 144:1). As God was faithful to train David in the use of physical weapons, He will teach you how to use your spiritual weapons.

It is more important that *we* know who we are and what we have in Christ Jesus than that the enemy knows it. Our tests and trials are designed to work this knowledge from just a mind belief into an inner sense of authority. Confidence in holding to, or standing firm, comes from our *inner* knowing that the words of Jesus are true and what He has said will come to pass. The peace of this inner authority is our foundation for defeating the enemy. When Satan sees that *we* know we can do everything because of Christ Jesus within, he will not argue with us for long.

Review your Isaiah 26:3 surfboard. How does this perfect peace come?

_____

_____

_____

How do having a steadfast mind and trusting God contribute to the effectiveness of our spiritual armor?

_____

_____

_____

_____

Explain the importance of realizing that there will be a spiritual battle and knowing that we are equipped to be victorious in that battle.

_____

_____

_____

_____

Action Steps I Can Take Today

When we are ill and the doctor writes us a prescription, we have a choice as to what we will do with that piece of paper. Some of us will take it home and wait to see if we'll get better without having to use it. Others of us will take it to the druggist immediately to get it filled.

In Philippians 4:4-8, the apostle Paul wrote us a prescription for becoming free from worry. Whenever we see the symptoms of anxiety appear in our lives, we can avoid this spiritual "dis-ease" by immediately applying Paul's counsel.

Memorize Philippians 4:4-7. Paul begins by telling us to "rejoice in the Lord"—who He is and what He has done for us. This expression of praise and thanksgiving will gentle us down, and others will be able to tell we believe the Lord is near in our problem situation.

How do you act when you are worried and upset? A friend said, "That's when I slam the cupboard doors and kick the cat." What happens to your gentleness when worry envelops you?

_____

_____

_____

_____

Continue to practice what we learned about rejoicing, praying and giving thanks in all situations. How many problems are we allowed to keep in our worry thoughts?

_____

_____

_____

_____

How many things are we to give to the Lord, and how are we to wrap them?

_____

_____

_____

_____

Remember our verses about thanksgiving? (Can you recite them from memory?) Why do you think giving thanks is important?

_____

_____

_____

_____

Paul's admonition means we are to literally present *all* our cares to God, even the small, seemingly silly things. I've asked Him to help me find car keys, the missing mate of my husband's socks, and the gift I'd stored somewhere. In some ways, His answers concerning the small things mean more to me than His answer concerning something large. How wonderful to have a heavenly Father who cares about even the little details of my life. Jesus said, "Whoever can be trusted with very little can also be trusted with much" (Luke 16:10). If we see God's faithfulness in the little things, our trust in Him for the bigger things will be made stronger.

Practice combining the things you have learned, beginning with expressing thanksgiving and praise, and then giving every care—large and small—to the Lord. Why not be bold enough to ask God to take care of a *little* thing that you had decided was too small for Him to be interested in? Remember to wrap your requests in thankfulness to God for His faithfulness.

The promise of Philippians 4:7 brings us back to the authority of the peace of God within us. Knowing we have Christ's authority within us makes us able to withstand the temptations of the enemy as he tries to manipulate us back into our old worry patterns. Remember, we don't battle against flesh and blood but against the spiritual forces of fear and worry. So we battle from the Spirit of Christ within us—God's Spirit against the spiritual forces of darkness.

John encouraged us, "The one who is in you is greater than the one who is in the world" (1 John 4:4). So if we hold to this truth and stand firm against the enemy, who will be victorious?

_____

_____

_____

_____

Some freedom-from-worriers tell me that they feel guilty when the peace of God comes. If the enemy can't use fear and worry, he will use guilt to try to move you out of the place of peace. The feeling-guilty former worriers say others accuse them of not caring because they're not fretting. How do you feel about being labeled by others as noncaring?

_____

_____

_____

_____

Can you live with yourself being at peace in the midst of a messy, problem situation? What are some of the challenges you can expect to face concerning your unwillingness to be pulled into anxiety?

_____

_____

_____

_____

If you're going to live free from worry, you will need to become accustomed to experiencing God's peace in the center of a storm. The Spirit of Christ within you will confirm the rightness of God's peace, but much of the world will not understand or appreciate your quiet confidence in the midst of trouble.

Practice doing what Paul admonished the Colossians: "*Let* the peace of Christ rule in your hearts" (Colossians 3:15, emphasis added). Don't let a sense of guilt draw you back into your old worry habit because it feels like genuine caring. In a troublesome situation, you can accomplish more with a peaceful heart than you ever can with the hurry and worry of a troubled heart.

Read 2 Corinthians 9:6-11. As we sow seed from what we have learned about becoming free from worry, what does God promise in verse 6?

_____

_____

_____

According to verse 7, how are we to share the blessings of the freedom from worry that God has given us?

_____

_____

_____

God is the provider, the life, and the multiplier of our freedom-from-worry seed. How does this Scripture encourage us to share with others as a way to receive even greater freedom in our own lives?

_____

_____

_____

Share with someone what you have learned from experience about the reality of being able to be free from worry, and then review the list of worries you made at the beginning of this study. How have you changed since you wrote the list?

_____

_____

_____

How would your list read now?

_____

_____

_____

_____

How do you want your list to read a year from now?

_____

_____

_____

_____

⇒ ✤ ⇐

Paul says that we can be confident of this: "That he who began a good work in you will carry it on to completion until the day of Christ Jesus" (Philippians 1:6). *A good work has begun.* Trust God to carry it on as you live the faith principles you have learned.

Each time I rewrite or teach the *Free from Worry* lessons, their truths sink deeper into my own heart. Thank you for allowing me to plant seeds in your lives. I pray that the planting has enriched your walk with God as much as it has mine. I'm looking forward to the day we meet face to face—either here or there or in the air!

FREE FROM WORRY LEADER'S GUIDE

The purpose of this leader's guide is to provide those willing to lead a group Bible study with additional material to make the study more effective. Each lesson has one or two exercises designed to increase participation and lead the group members into a more conscious awareness of the effects of worry on their lives.

Each of the exercises are designed to introduce the study and emphasize the theme of the chapter. When two exercises are suggested, it is up to your discretion whether to use them both. Time will probably be the deciding factor.

If the group is larger than six members, you may want to break into smaller groups for the discussion time so that all will have an adequate opportunity to share. As the lessons proceed, the exercises will invite more personal sharing. Keep these two important points in mind:

1. Involve each member of the group in the discussion when at all possible. Some may be too shy or new to the Bible study experience. Be sensitive to their needs and encourage them to answer simple questions that do not require personal information or biblical knowledge. As they get more comfortable in the group, they will probably share more often.

2. Make a commitment with the group members that what is shared in the discussion times and prayer requests must be kept in strictest confidence.

After each lesson, be prepared to pray with those who have special needs or concerns. Emphasize the truth of God's Word as you minister to the group members; expect Him to heal the sin of worry and set them free to be who they truly are in Christ.

ᴍᴀᴋɪɴɢ ᴀ ᴄʜᴏɪᴄᴇ

Objective

To help group members understand that each of us has the choice of whether to obey the Lord or to do our own thing.

Preparation

EXERCISE
You will need a whiteboard, chalkboard or flip chart and felt-tip pens or chalk. Write "Daily Choices" and "Life-Altering Choices" across the top of the board or chart and draw a line between the titles, leaving room for answers under each.

DISCUSSION
Familiarize yourself with the discussion questions included in the following "Group Participation" section, or choose which questions in this week's study you want to discuss with the group. Note that there might not be time to discuss every question, so modify or adapt this discussion guide as it fits the needs of your group. Additional discussion/action steps are also provided to help stimulate further discussion if you have the time.

Group Participation

EXERCISE
Display the chart you have prepared. Have group members suggest choices they make on a daily basis, (for example, getting out of bed or staying in bed, what to eat for breakfast, exercising or watching TV, having devotional time, or leaving earlier for work). Discuss the consequences of these choices. Also list the life-altering choices that one makes—for example, how to spend and/or save money, whether to move or stay put, whether to marry or not, what occupational choices to pursue, and so forth. Discuss

the consequences of making poor choices. If no one has suggested the choice to follow and/or obey the Lord, lead the discussion to that conclusion. Relate to how we must daily choose to obey the Lord.

DISCUSSION

1. Invite a volunteer to read Genesis 3:1-9 aloud. Discuss the following questions (or the ones you chose) from the "A Closer Look at God's Truth" section:

    •   How did Satan draw Eve into a discussion about her choice?

    •   What did Satan imply about the character of God as he encouraged Eve to question God's motives?

    •   According to verse 6, what reasons for disobeying God did Eve give?

    •   What did Adam and Eve do when they heard God walking in the Garden? Why did they do it?

    •   Why do you think God asked Adam and Eve where they were (see verse 9)? Didn't He know?

2. Read Luke 10:38-42 aloud. Discuss the following questions (or the ones you chose) from the "A Closer Look at My Own Heart" section:

    •   One man quipped, "Even God would worry if He watched the evening news." Would He? How do you think God wants us to respond (see Matthew 24:6)?

    •   What does Martha say to Jesus about Mary's ignoring all the preparations that seemed to need immediate attention?

    •   Think of some situations where you have felt that God didn't understand your circumstances. Identify some times when you pointed out to Him the need as you saw it, expecting that somehow, once you explained, He would do what you thought needed to be done. What happened?

    •   In His love for Martha, Jesus revealed to her a need in her life that went much deeper than her distress about serving. What did He want her to see?

- In Deuteronomy 8:3, God said to the Israelites, "Man does not live on bread alone but on every word that comes from the mouth of the Lord." How does Jesus illustrate this truth in His sharing with Martha and Mary?

ADDITIONAL DISCUSSION/ACTION STEPS

1. In what ways did the members identify with Martha? With Mary? (You may need to get the discussion started by sharing your own answer to this question.)

2. Invite volunteers to react to the "Action Steps" they were to take at the conclusion of the lesson. Invite volunteers to share if they found the activity hurtful, helpful or hard. Remind the group members to keep their responses to this activity for use in the next chapter's Action Steps.

Note: Instruct group members to keep the lists of their present worries throughout the study to be returned to in the final week.

$\mathscr{I}$DENTIFYING WORRY

Objective

To help group members understand the damage to their abundant life that is caused by worry and to identify the fears behind their worries.

Preparation

EXERCISE 1

Prepare a short list of some of the silliest worries you have ever had or have heard from others.

EXERCISE 2

Write the following quote on a piece of poster board, or on the whiteboard, chalkboard or flipchart:

> *Worry-motivated praying might be described as prayer to the wrong god.*

Prepare an example of worry-motivated prayer to break the ice and help group members come up with their own examples.

DISCUSSION

Familiarize yourself with the discussion questions included in the following "Group Participation" section, or choose which questions in this week's study you want to discuss with the group.

Group Participation

EXERCISE 1

Invite group members to share the silliest worry they have ever heard of. Begin the sharing with one or two of your own that you have prepared ahead of time.

EXERCISE 2

Invite group members to respond to the quote: "Worry-motivated praying might be described as prayer to the wrong god." Ask for specific examples of what might be a worry-motivated prayer. Take one example and discuss how a worry-motivated prayer can be turned into a more effective prayer that results in peace for the one who is worried.

DISCUSSION

1. Discuss the following questions (or the ones you chose) from the "A Closer Look at God's Truth" section:

    •   Does worry add abundance to your life, or does it take abundance away? List some of the ways that worry steals, kills and destroys in your life.

    •   Can you tell when you are worried? How does it affect you?

    •   What are some of the reasons you use to justify your worry?

    •   Do you remember how Jesus said to Martha, "Martha, Martha . . . you are worried and upset about many things" (Luke 10:41)? Read John 11:5 to find out Jesus' motive for addressing this problem in her life. Now refer back to John 10:10. Why does Jesus want us to be free from worry in our lives?

    •   What problems are you trying to solve with your own reasoning? How many "paralytics" are you struggling to help walk when they need to be brought on the "mat of faith" to Jesus?

2. Discuss the following questions from the "A Closer Look at My Own Heart" section:

    •   How many of our worries whirl around the fear of some embarrassment coming to us through our own actions or the actions of those who are connected to us in some way? Identify such a fear in your collection of worried thoughts. How does this fear affect your thought life?

    •   How does this fear affect your actions?

- Why do you hesitate to give God all your cares?

- Identify a situation where fear and pride have combined to make you feel eaten up with worry.

ADDITIONAL DISCUSSION/ACTION STEPS

1. Discuss how fear is related to worry.

2. Ask group members to share their definitions of worry that they wrote in the Action Steps section. Invite volunteers to share what they learned from doing this activity.

THREE

CALLING A SIN A SIN

Objective

To help group members identify worry as sin and to develop strategies to overcome the sin of worry.

Preparation

EXERCISE

Have one large piece of poster board or newsprint and pens available for every three to four members of your group and tape or tacks to display the papers on the walls. Also have a whiteboard, chalkboard or flipchart available to summarize their definition into one.

DISCUSSION

Familiarize yourself with the discussion questions included in the following "Group Participation" section, or choose which questions in this week's study you want to discuss with the group.

Group Participation

EXERCISE

Have volunteers read the following verses: Genesis 3:1-7; James 1:14-15; 1 John 2:16. Discuss the steps that lead to sin as illustrated in these verses: *Temptations that appeal to fleshly desires, the lust of the eyes and personal pride.*

If you have a group of six or more members, divide the group into smaller groups of three or four. Instruct each small group to come up with a definition of sin. After a couple of minutes of discussion, have each group share their definition. Summarize their definitions into one common definition and write it on the whiteboard, chalkboard or flipchart. Discuss with the participants how worry is a sin according to the definition the group developed.

DISCUSSION

1. Invite a volunteer to read Matthew 6:25-34 aloud. Discuss the following questions (or the ones you chose) from the "A Closer Look at God's Truth" section:

    - About what things did Jesus tell us not to worry?

    - Do you think worry adds to the quality or length of your life? One woman explained, "The things I worry about never happen, so I see worry as kind of a preventative." What do you think of her reasoning?

    - The command of Jesus concerning worry comes from His love for us. He speaks to us about worry as we might speak to a friend reaching for a poisonous drink: "Stop! Don't touch that!" If Jesus says "do not" and we do, have we been disobedient? Why or why not?

    - Jesus never gave us a "do not" without giving a positive direction for us to take instead of the forbidden one. According to Matthew 6:33, what did Jesus tell us to seek first? What did He promise will follow our seeking God's way first?

    - In Matthew 6:34, Jesus told us not to worry about tomorrow. He didn't mean we are not to think about tomorrow or make future plans, but the motivation for our planning is not to be anxiety. In these days, why does it seem unrealistic not to worry about the future?

2. Discuss the following questions (or the ones you chose) from the "A Closer Look at My Own Heart" section:

    - When our hearts are full of worry and our heads full of unproductive thoughts whirling around a center of hidden fear, are our meditations acceptable in the sight of One who said, "Do not worry"? Why or why not?

    - What kind of words do you hear spoken by worried people?

    - How would your meditations and conversations change if you began to focus more on the realities of God's kingdom and less on the uncertainties of man's world?

- As honestly as you can, describe the fears that keep you from trusting God and that keep you centering on your problems rather than on God's faithfulness.

ADDITIONAL DISCUSSION/ACTION STEPS

1. What are some practical ways that we can implement Jesus' instruction in Matthew 6:33, particularly when we are tempted to worry? Lead group members to suggest actions such as *spending time in God's Word, praying, having a prayer partner to keep you accountable,* and so forth.

2. Encourage group members to memorize Matthew 6:33 and to recite it whenever they are tempted to worry. If there is time, spend some time as a group memorizing the verse by writing it on the board and then erasing a word or two at a time until they are reciting it from memory.

FOUR

Making your VOTE COUNT

Objective

To help group members understand the Source of strength to be free from worry. Also to provide an opportunity for those who have not yet accepted Jesus as Lord and Savior of their lives.

Preparation

EXERCISE

Do you know of a member of your group or congregation who has over-come an addiction, a bad habit or a besetting sin? Enlist that person to prepare a brief testimony of her struggle and ultimate victory over that sinful behavior. Or perhaps you can prepare a testimony about your own experience in overcoming a sin.

DISCUSSION

Familiarize yourself with the discussion questions included in the follow-ing "Group Participation" section, or choose which questions in this week's study you want to discuss with the group. There might also be group members who have accepted the Lord this week, as this week's study invited those who have not yet received Christ as Savior and Lord to do so. Provide an opportunity to allow them to make a public commitment. Approach this session with a lot of prayer. Also be prepared with follow-up materials and contacts.

Group Participation

EXERCISE

Have the person (or you) share the testimony about overcoming sin. Em-phasize that overcoming a habit or addiction that has been years in the making may take some time and in fact may still be a daily choice to resist the temptations. Especially emphasize Philippians 4:13 and the Lord's part in overcoming sin. If at all possible, have the person (or yourself) share some other Scripture verses and actions that have helped.

DISCUSSION

1. Discuss the following questions (or the ones you chose) from the "A Closer Look at God's Truth" section:

    · In his letter to the Colossians, Paul wrote of the mystery that has been revealed to the saints—those who have placed their faith in Jesus Christ. What does this verse tell us about our being much more than *only human*?

    · When a problem comes (no matter its size or severity), do you react out of your human nature, or do you respond out of the Christ-life within you?

    · Read Hebrews 4:14-15. Did Jesus ever face worry temptations like we do? The Bible says Jesus was tempted in every way, just as we are. There's no note in the margin saying "except for worry." So if Jesus was tempted to worry, just like we are, and "yet was without sin" (verse 15), what does that tell us about the worry-resisting ability of His life in us?

    · Now read Hebrews 2:17-18. The writer explained how "in every way" Jesus had to be made like us in order to face and defeat all the temptations and destructions Satan brings against us. According to verse 18, how easy was it for Jesus to face the temptations (including the temptation to worry) without giving in to sin?

    · The closing words of verse 18 encourage us as we face our temptations: "He is able to help those who are being tempted." How do these words fit with Paul's description of the "mystery" we can have within us?

2. Discuss the following questions from the "A Closer Look at My Own Heart" section:

- How do you suppose Paul had arrived at this place in his life?

- What does the use of the word "learned" imply about the process involved in coming to trust the power of the life of Christ in us?

- In Philippians 4:13, how did Paul explain his ability to be content?

- What is the state of your heart right now? Are you willing to learn (even if it seems impossible) how to take charge of the worry temptations that draw you into sin?

Additional Discussion/Action Steps

1. Invite a volunteer to read Isaiah 12:2 aloud. Ask the group members if they believe this verse. If so, why?

2. Read Hebrews 4:14-18 aloud. Ask the group members what comfort they receive from these verses. What challenges do they receive?

3. Read Philippians 4:11-13. Invite volunteers to share how they have experienced this kind of contentment in times of want or plenty.

4. Encourage group members to memorize Isaiah 26:3 and 1 Corinthians 10:13.

Note: Invite any new believers to stay after the meeting to discuss the life-changing step they have taken and what it means. Give them the materials you have collected. Also extend the invitation to become a believer to the group members at the end of this session in case someone else is ready to make this commitment now.

Having a New Mind

Objective

To help group members understand that when we asked Jesus Christ to dwell within, He gave us new minds, and that we must cultivate our new way of thinking.

Preparation

EXERCISE

Collect a stack of popular magazines and newspapers that contain articles or advertisements that demonstrate how the media preys on our minds, causing us to be dissatisfied with our present situations or to be anxious about our futures.

DISCUSSION

Familiarize yourself with the discussion questions included in the following "Group Participation" section, or choose which questions in this week's study you want to discuss with the group.

Group Participation

EXERCISE

Invite the group members to form groups of two or three. Provide each group with a couple of magazines or newspapers. Instruct them to browse through the magazines and newspapers to find articles or advertisements that demonstrate how the media and our culture entice us to become dissatisfied about our present situations or anxious about our futures. Give the groups about five minutes to find their best example, and then have the whole group come together to share what they have found. As each small group shares their example, discuss how the world tempts us to be dissatisfied and anxious. If time permits, discuss the following questions about each example:

1. What does this ad or article demonstrate?

2. How could this example cause our minds to become dissatisfied or anxious?

3. What did you learn from this week's lesson that could help you overcome the dissatisfaction or worry brought about by reading this article or ad?

Conclude by reading John 14:27, and then invite group members to share how they have discovered this biblical truth in their own lives.

DISCUSSION

1. Begin the discussion time by asking group members to share what they learned about the humanity of Jesus Christ from this week's lesson and how they can use that knowledge to better deal with the temptation to worry.

2. Discuss the following questions (or the ones you chose) from the "A Closer Look at God's Truth" section:

   • Contrast life according to the Spirit with life according to the sinful nature as described in verses 6-8. Where does a mind set on fear and worry fit in this description?

   • What are some ways a change in your thinking would affect your actions?

   • If you practiced this, believing it was best because it is God's way, what would happen to your fretting about past hurts, worrying about running into that person who doesn't like you, and so forth?

   • What are some of the attitudes and actions you know God wants you to exhibit but that you brush aside, choosing to stay with your old flesh-nature patterns?

   • To break the power of sinful thought patterns, we have to replace them with God-patterned thinking. What are some of the ways you know you will have to think differently to break the worry thought patterns in your mind?

2. Ask the group what they wrote in response to the question, "How does your heart respond to the thought, *Worry is a type of spiritual cancer that needs to be dealt with in my life? Do you care enough to do what must be done?*"

ADDITIONAL DISCUSSION/ACTION STEPS

1. The group was asked to consider the sin of worry like a cancer that has invaded our minds. How did that change their perspective on how to deal with sin in their lives?

2. What can they do to remove this cancer of sin?

3. Invite group members to share a verse from this week's lesson that was particularly helpful in helping them deal with the sin of worry. Have them explain why they chose that verse. Encourage members to memorize those Scriptures that will add to their arsenal against temptation.

SIX

SPINNING DAYDREAMS, FEEDING NIGHTMARES

Objective

To help group members discover the tools and thought processes to resist temptation.

Preparation

EXERCISE 1

Before the meeting, prepare (or purchase) a beautifully arranged plate of colorful fresh fruits and vegetables. Also prepare a bowl displaying bland-looking junk food, such as, potato chips, marshmallows, French fries, cookies, etc.—just make it look as bland and uninviting as possible. If you want to share the *good* food after the meeting, provide napkins and small plates.

EXERCISE 2

Prepare a chart on the whiteboard, chalkboard or flipchart by writing "Worries"; "What Can I Do"; "What Only God Can Do" across the top of the chart divide by a line between each, leaving room underneath each heading to write group members' responses.

DISCUSSION

Familiarize yourself with the discussion questions included in the following "Group Participation" section, or choose which questions in this week's study you want to discuss with the group.

Group Participation

EXERCISE 1

As you begin the meeting, bring out the plates of food and display them on a table. Begin the exercise by asking the following:

1. Which is the most attractive display of food? Why? (Hopefully members will choose the plate of fruits and vegetables, but if someone doesn't, allow that person to explain their reasons.)

2. Which are the healthiest choices?

3. Why should we choose to eat the fresh fruits and vegetables over the junk food?

4. How does this relate to making wise choices for our thoughts to dwell on?

5. What might be some of those healthy choices of thoughts for our minds to dwell on during troubling times?

EXERCISE 2

Display the chart you have prepared. Invite group members to suggest some common worries we all face, and then write them down the right-hand column. When you have a list of about four or five items, ask the group members to consider the things they can personally do to alleviate each worry. For example, if someone has suggested a health concern such as an unusual pain, ask if there is anything we can do about this worry. The answer might be, *We should make an appointment with the doctor to have it checked.*

Next, discuss some worries about this circumstance that might take their thoughts captive and rob them of their peace concerning this circumstance. (Answers could include *that we are going to be seriously ill* or *who would take care of our children if something would happen to us*). Continue down the list as time allows. Conclude by having volunteers read each of the "surfboard verses" from the previous week's Action Steps.

DISCUSSION

1. Have someone in the group read James 1:2-4 aloud. Discuss the following questions (or the ones you chose) from the "A Closer Look at God's Truth" section:

   · What do you think of James's challenge to us concerning how we face our trials?

   · Think about how your anxiety compares to a surfer's delight. How is it possible for you to consider a trial that causes worry as a source of joy?

- How do you respond to the need for patient practice in order to bring your worry under control?

- Remembering that no temptation can come our way except what God allows and that He has promised to make a way for us to bear it, how can waves of worry prove these truths?

- How can worry waves show the reliability of your Scripture surfboards (memorized verses)?

2. Read James 1:12-15 aloud to the group. Discuss the following questions (or the ones you chose) from the "A Closer Look at My Own Heart" section:

- How does this passage show that temptation is normal for the Christian?

- Why does breaking down strongholds of worry and taking captive every vain imagination require endurance? What kind of endurance does freeing ourselves from worry require of you personally?

- Why can we resist Satan?

- Identify a recent "hook, line and sinker" scenario in which you imagined a possible problem and solution. How much mind time did you spend on it?

- What tempts you to accept worry as a necessary part of your life?

ADDITIONAL DISCUSSION/ACTION STEPS

Write on the whiteboard, chalkboard or flipchart the group members suggestions for tools we might use to resist temptation (for instance, *prayer, Scripture memory, an accountability partner*). Invite volunteers to share ways that they have successfully dealt with the temptation to worry.

SEVEN

Thanking God Always

Objective

To give group members practice in expressing thankfulness in all circumstances.

Preparation

EXERCISE 1

Gather plain paper and pencils or pens for use during the exercise. Obtain a timer or watch with a second hand and a simple prize for the winner of the competition, such as a small note pad, a candle or a candy bar.

EXERCISE 2

Find someone—preferably one of the group members—who could lead the group in singing two or three praise and worship songs, or obtain a worship CD and a CD player. This will be used at the end of the session.

DISCUSSION

Familiarize yourself with the discussion questions included in the following "Group Participation" section, or choose which questions in this week's study you want to discuss with the group. Note that if you choose to do exercise 2 above, you will want to leave about 10 minutes at the end of the session for a time of praise and worship, so choose just the number of questions that you think your group will be able to discuss during the meeting time.

Group Participation

EXERCISE 1

Give each group member a sheet of plain paper and a pencil or pen. Introduce the activity by asking each member to share one thing he or she is thankful for at this moment. Tell the group that they will be having a one-minute thank-a-thon. Give them one minute to write down as many things that they are thankful for that they have encountered and experienced during the last 24 hours.

Before they begin, have them write "God," "Jesus," and "salvation" at the top of their lists, as those are probably things everyone will write. Encourage them to be creative about the *thankful-fors* that are specific to their own lives. Set the timer for one minute as you tell them to begin.

After one minute, instruct the members to stop writing. Discover who has the most items on her list. Invite that person to read the list. Discuss what he or she has learned from the exercise.

DISCUSSION

1. Discuss the following questions (or the ones you chose) from the "A Closer Look at God's Truth" section:

   • What worry problem are you focusing on solving, thinking that when you finally get it taken care of you'll be able to concentrate on your relationship with the Lord again? How do you feel about His urging you to concentrate on Him now?

   • Name some of the things about God that are worthy of our rejoicing, regardless of how difficult our immediate circumstances may be.

   • Why do we find it hard to obey this command when we're worried and troubled about many things?

   • How could rejoicing be used as a spiritual weapon against worry?

   • What do you think happens in us when we make the sacrificial effort to show thankfulness to God?

2. Discuss the following questions (or the ones you chose) from the "A Closer Look at My Own Heart" section:

   • Why is practicing the principles related to being set free from worry so important?

- Write an example of how you might talk to yourself to bring your soul into obediently (not necessarily "feelingly") offering a sacrifice of thanksgiving to God.

- Why do you feel it is too hard for you to give the sacrifice of thanksgiving?

- Do you feel justified in holding on to your fear, your anger, your worry? Why?

- Look again at David's words in Psalms 34 and 103 and at the behavior of Paul and Silas in Acts 16. Reread Philippians 4:13. How was Paul enabled to give thanks? How can you? Will you choose to do it?

ADDITIONAL DISCUSSION/ACTION STEPS

1. Ask if there is anyone who would like to share an experience in which he or she discovered Jesus' yoke is easy and His burden is light. (If no one volunteers, share your own experience.)

2. Ask if anyone has experienced that approaching a difficult time with thanksgiving has changed his or her reaction to a difficult time.

EXERCISE 2

Begin the time of worship by inviting group members to pray brief sentence prayers of thanksgiving to the Lord. End this time of worship by singing two or three of the praise songs you have selected.

Note: Remind group members to bring their "worry lists" from the first week's study to next week's meeting.

*S*TAYING FREE

Objective

To challenge group members to continue to resist the sin of worry and to walk in the freedom from worry that only the Lord provides.

Preparation

EXERCISE 1

Remind group members during the week to bring their worry lists from the first week's study.

EXERCISE 2

Once again, invite someone—preferably one of the group members—to lead the group in singing two or three praise and worship songs, or obtain a worship CD and a CD player. This will be used at the end of the session.

Discussion

Familiarize yourself with the discussion questions included in the following "Group Participation" section, or choose which questions in this week's study you want to discuss with the group. Again, note that if you choose to do exercise 2 above, you will want to leave about 10 minutes at the end of the session for a time of praise and worship, so choose just the number of questions that you think your group will be able to discuss during the meeting time.

Group Participation

EXERCISE 1

Instruct the group members to read their list of worries from the first week's session. Invite each group member to share how his or her perspective on worry has changed over the past eight weeks of study. Discuss the changes he or she has experienced over the past weeks.

DISCUSSION

1. Begin by inviting volunteers to share a favorite Scripture verse that they have found especially meaningful during the past weeks. Ask them to explain why that chosen verse is so meaningful. You might begin the sharing with one of your own favorite verses.

2. Discuss the following questions (or the ones you chose) from the "A Closer Look at God's Truth" section:

    -   What do the words "free indeed" tell us about the kind of freedom from worry Jesus intends for us to experience?

    -   What is the difference between having an occasional worry-free time and a lifestyle that refuses to entertain worry thoughts?

    -   What are some of the ways worry hinders your Christian walk and entangles your thinking?

    -   Review Matthew 6:33. How does this verse tell us we are to keep our worry butterflies "in formation"?

    -   Read Hebrews 12:2-3. What do these verses tell us about the probability of our becoming weary and losing heart at times as we strive to be free from worry?

3. Discuss the following questions (or the ones you chose) from the "A Closer Look at My Own Heart" section:

    -   Does it make you somewhat fearful and anxious to hear how your freedom from worry will be challenged? Why or why not?

    -   How does Ephesians 6:12 describe our battle? Since our flesh is helpless to fight spiritual forces, why is it important for us to recognize the power of the Spirit of Christ in us?

- Reread Ephesians 6:14-17. List the weapons that are identified as protection for us to use in the spiritual battles we will face. Beside each weapon, write how Jesus is each of the weapons.

- How do having a steadfast mind and trusting God contribute to the effectiveness of our spiritual armor?

- Explain the importance of realizing that there will be a spiritual battle and knowing that we are equipped to be victorious in that battle.

ADDITIONAL DISCUSSION/ACTION STEPS

1. Ask the members what is the most amazing truth they have learned from this study.

2. Ask how that truth will impact their lives.

3. Discuss what they can do to maintain their freedom from worry.

EXERCISE 2

Close this final session with a time of praise and worship. Begin with a time of group prayer and conclude with singing praise and worship songs.

WHAT IS AGLOW INTERNATIONAL?

———◇◇◇———

From one nation to 172 worldwide...
From one fellowship to more than 4,600...
From 100 people to more than 17 million...

———◇◇◇———

Aglow International has experienced phenomenal growth since its inception more than 40 years ago. In 1967, four women from the state of Washington prayed for a way to reach out to other Christian women in simple fellowship, free from denominational boundaries.

———◇◇◇———

The first meeting held in Seattle, Washington, USA, drew more than 100 women to a local hotel. From that modest beginning, Aglow International has become one of the largest intercultural, interdenominational Christian organizations in the world.

———◇◇◇———

Each year, an estimated 17 million people are ministered to through Aglow's local fellowship meetings, Bible studies, support groups, retreats, conferences and various outreaches. From the inner city to the upper echelons, from the next door neighbor to the corporate executive, Aglow seeks to minister to the felt needs of women and men around the world.

———◇◇◇———

Christian women and men find Aglow a "safe place" to grow spiritually and begin to discover and use the gifts, talents and abilities God has given them. Aglow offers excellent leadership training and varied opportunities to develop those leadership skills.

———◇◇◇———

Undergirding the evangelistic thrust of the ministry is an emphasis on prayer, which has led to an active prayer network linking six continents. The vast prayer power available through Aglow women and men around the world is being used by God to influence countless lives in families, communities, cities and nations.

AGLOW'S MISSION STATEMENT IS . . .

- To help restore and mobilize women and men around the world

- To promote gender reconciliation in the Body of Christ as God designed

- To amplify awareness of global concerns from a biblical perspective

AGLOW'S THREE MANDATES

1. To promote gender reconciliation between male and female in the Body of Christ as God designed.

2. To answer God's call to minister to the Muslim people, while bringing awareness of the basic theological differences between Islam and Christianity.

3. To stand in loving support for Israel and the Jewish people, while helping to bring awareness to the Body of Christ concerning God's plans and purposes for those people He calls the "apple of His eye."

AGLOW MINISTERS IN . . .

Albania, Angola, Anguilla, Antigua, Argentina, Aruba, Australia, Austria, Bahamas, Bahrain, Barbados, Belarus, Belgium, Belize, Benin, Bermuda, Bolivia, Botswana, Brazil, Britain, Bulgaria, Burkina Faso, Cameroon, Canada, Chile, China, Colombia, Congo (Dem. Rep. of), Congo (Rep. of), Costa Rica, Côte d'Ivoire, Cuba, Curaçao, Czech Republic, Denmark, Djibouti, Dominica, Dominican Republic, Ecuador, Egypt, El Salvador, Equatorial Guinea, Estonia, Ethiopia, Faroe Islands, Fiji, Finland, France, Gabon, the Gambia, Germany, Ghana, Grand Cayman, Greece, Grenada, Guam, Guatemala, Guinea, Guyana, Haiti, Honduras, Hungary, Iceland, India, Indonesia, Ireland, Israel, Jamaica, Japan, Kenya, Korea, Kyrgyzstan, Latvia, Lithuania, Malawi, Malaysia, Mali, Mauritius, Mexico, Mongolia, Mozambique, Myanmar, Nepal, Netherlands, New Zealand, Nicaragua, Niger, Nigeria, Norway, Oman, Pakistan, Panama, Papua New Guinea, Peru, Philippines, Portugal, Puerto Rico, Romania, Russia, Rwanda, Samoa, Samoa (American), Scotland, Senegal, Serbia, Sierra Leone, Singapore, South Africa, Spain, Sri Lanka, St. Kitts, St. Lucia, St. Maartan, St. Vincent, Sudan, Suriname, Sweden, Switzerland, Tajikistan, Tanzania, Thailand, Togo, Tonga, Trinidad/ Tobago, Turks & Caicos Islands, Uganda, Ukraine, United States, Uruguay, Uzbekistan, Venezuela, Vietnam, Virgin Islands (American), Virgin Islands (British), Wales, Yugoslavia, Zambia, Zimbabwe, and other nations.

To find your nearest Aglow Fellowship, call or write us at:

P.O. Box 1749, Edmonds, WA 98020-1749
Phone: 425-775-7282 or 1-800-793-8126
Fax: 425-778-9615 / Email: aglow@aglow.org
Website: http://www.aglow.org/

WOMEN OF THE WORD
BIBLE STUDY SERIES

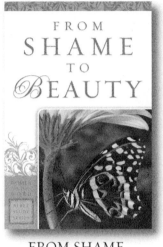

FROM SHAME
TO BEAUTY
Marie Powers
ISBN 978.08307.52355

BUILDING BETTER
RELATIONSHIPS
Bobbie Yagel
ISBN 978.08307.52362

A WOMAN AFTER
GOD'S HEART
Eadie Goodboy
ISBN 978.08307.52331

CAPTIVATED
BY GOD
Eadie Goodboy & Agnes Lawless
ISBN 978.08307.54953